A Brief Sketch of the Establishment of the Anglican Church in India

A Brief Sketch

OF

THE ESTABLISHMENT

OF THE

ANGLICAN CHURCH IN INDIA.

BY

MAJOR-GENERAL PARLBY, C.B.

LONDON:

SKEFFINGTON AND SOUTHWELL, 192 PICCADILLY.

1851.

TO THE

VENERABLE ARCHDEACON ROBINSON, D.D

MASTER OF THE TEMPLE,

THE FRIEND OF BISHOP HEBER,

THIS HUMBLE ATTEMPT TO DESCRIBE THE DIFFICULTIES

WHICH ATTENDED THE PROGRESS OF

THE ANGLICAN CHURCH IN INDIA,

IS, BY HIS PERMISSION,

MOST RESPECTFULLY DEDICATED.

PREFACE.

A BRIEF sketch of the Anglican Church in India by a Major-general ! ! ! What can a military man know of the history of the Church militant ?

This is a reflection which will readily suggest itself to the European critic, and we are prepared to answer it; whilst to those who have resided in India there is no necessity for explanation.

Previous to the arrival of the first Anglican Bishop, upwards of thirty-six years ago, the

existing Church Establishment was of a semi-
military, semi-clerical description. Even after
Dr. Middleton had commenced his valuable
labours, it took some years to mould it
into shape, to define the strict limits of con-
flicting authorities, and to trace the broad
line which was *in future* to separate the
former military chaplain from the interference of governors and commanders-in-chief,
and to place him under the immediate control of his legitimate superior. There seems
no valid reason, therefore, why a layman
should be precluded from attempting a slight
sketch, for it professes to be nothing more, of
the infancy, the earlier years, and the maturity
of the Anglican Church in our Indian possession; to give a faint outline of some of the
struggles it had to endure; and to record its
ultimate triumph. The object proposed is

simply to deliver "a plain unvarnished tale," stating broad facts, and drawing from them such inferences as may serve to explain the anomalous position in which the Church was formerly placed. It would be presumption to venture on any discussion of the peculiar tenets of the Anglican Episcopal Church, or to touch on those nice doctrinal and theological questions, which, to be properly handled, must be undertaken by those who, from their sacred calling, and from the studies incidental to their profession, are fitly qualified to argue and explain them.

The subject of Church discipline has been but slightly touched upon, as this has been very ably discussed in an excellent little work by the Rev. William Whitehead, on the "Established Church in India," which has afforded many useful hints in compiling the following sketch.

This brief explanation of the object of the accompanying little work will, it is hoped, sufficiently denote its character. We will merely add, that it was originally intended for a periodical, but having grown beyond the usual limits of an article, is published in its present form.

THE CHURCH OF ENGLAND
IN INDIA.

"I AM VERY ANXIOUS UPON THIS SUBJECT, FROM
A KNOWLEDGE THAT RELIGIOUS INSTRUCTION IS
THE GREATEST SUPPORT AND AID TO MILITARY
DISCIPLINE AND ORDER."

These are remarkable words of a remarkable per-
sonage, "the foremost man of all the world." Happy
are we to place them at the head of this work,
because they afford a convincing proof that amidst
those fierce conflicts, where "the horse mocketh at
fear, and is not affrighted, where he swalloweth the
ground with fierceness and rage, and saith among
the trumpets, Ha, ha! and smelleth the battle afar
off, the thunder of the captains, and the shouting,"
the DUKE OF WELLINGTON did not lose sight of
those eternal truths, the observance of which is alike
essential to the happiness of the soldier as of the
citizen. We contemplate them as a noble example
of the respect paid to the established religion of his

B

country by one whose high reputation elevated him equally above the scowl of the Pharisee or the sneer of the Infidel. Starting with, it must be acknowledged, such impartial testimony in favour of that Church to the enduring interests of which our humble labours are principally dedicated, we do not feel that we owe any apology to the general reader for placing before him some brief particulars of the progress of the Anglo-Indian establishment in the sunny regions of the East.

There has been, more especially of late years, no lack of writers on the general history of British India. Every circumstance connected with its politics, its literature, its antiquities, its natural history, its commercial and fiscal interests, its military achievements, and its progress in civilisation, has occupied the pens of various writers of no ordinary talent. Nor are we without honourable records of its most distinguished men, whether they have shone in the council-chamber, on the bench, or in the tented field. Yet amid all this variety of scientific research, of critical investigation, and of popular information, the Christian, whose contemplations are steadily fixed on those brighter scenes which are "eternal in the heavens," will discover that there is one thing wanting, and that by far the most precious and the most important of all. If we are of those who admit true religion to be the " be-all, and the end-all "—to be the keystone of the arch on which the whole framework of society hinges, and without which there can be no

solid foundation for contentment here, nor for hope
hereafter—then shall we be the more readily disposed
to inquire how far our country has fulfilled the high
duties imposed upon her, in conveying the pure and
serene light of Christianity to the lands · that were
under the shadow of darkness and the baneful do-
minion of idolatry. To such, then, as derive real
pleasure from contemplating the ark of Christ's
Church floating over the distant waters, and triumph-
antly surmounting the waves of this troublesome
world, we address ourselves.

To use the elegant language of Lamartine,—a writer
who, notwithstanding the strong poetical cast of his
mind, often surprises us by those brilliant coruscations
which his genius throws on the swift current that is
hurrying away the thoughts of earth, with its trifles,
and vanity, and sorrows, and sins, into the everlasting
ocean of eternity :—

" There is good sense, but with that good sense there
is virtue ; and it is impossible to reside in England for
any length of time without discovering it. The source
of that public virtue is the *religious feeling* with which
that people is endowed more than many others. A
divine feeling of practical religious liberty has developed
itself at the present moment, under a hundred forms,
amongst them. Every one has a temple of God, where
every one can recognise the light of reason, and adore
that God, and serve Him with his brethren in the sincerity and in the independence of his faith."

The merely superficial inquirer into ecclesiastical

history may, perchance, have been led to consider
the limited Church of British India as on too narrow
a scale to occupy his serious attention. He may
have viewed it as but a minnow amongst the tritons
—an object of minor importance in comparison with
those startling incidents which have at times shaken
the whole frame of society in Christendom, those
fierce conflicts of opinion, thôse bold assertions of
doctrine and discipline, the enforcing of which has
led to the block and to the stake, has disturbed the
minds of sincere Christians, and from the earliest
times has fretted and agitated the great European
community.

Should such a one in his cursory reading discover
that in 1756 Captain Lieutenant Mapletoft, of the
1st Company of Militia, was on the Sabbath-day the
Reverend Mr. Mapletoft, the solitary chaplain to the
Presidency of Calcutta, he will probably smile at
this pantomimic exchange of the helmet and the
sword of the soldier for the band and the academic
gown of the clergyman. After a lapse of half a
century, another anomaly might occasion his surprise. Amidst the universal marks of respect, and
the general mourning, which testified the feelings of
the European community to the memory of the
Marquis Cornwallis, he would learn that a funeral
service was performed at the churches of all the
Presidencies in India. In pursuance of this object,
the Governor of Bombay, Mr. Duncan, who had been
one of the early *protégés* of the deceased nobleman,

and who, in return for the patronage and promotion he had received, was anxious to show all possible honour to his memory, directed a funeral sermon to be preached at the church of St. Thomas. And to whom did he resort for this purpose ?—To the chaplain, of course. No, to Sir James Mackintosh, *the Recorder*, of whom he requested, as a personal favour, that he would compose the discourse which was to be delivered on the occasion. The Edinburgh Reviewer, we are told, readily complied with the wish thus expressed. He composed a very elegant sermon, which, his biographer informs us, was not less remarkable for the address with which the fullest praise is given to the generous and useful qualities of the deceased without the exaggeration which in like cases it is so difficult to avoid, than for the skilful mode in which the notorious misfortunes of his public life were touched upon. The worthy ecclesiastic whose legitimate province had been thus rudely intruded upon, would appear to have been well content to figure in the borrowed plumes of " the great Northern Light ;" for we learn that this sermon, which was much admired, was published at the time *under the name of the Senior Presidency Chaplain*. Imagine the sensation that would be caused in some quarters on discovering that a discourse which was delivered from the pulpit of a collegiate church, and which subsequently obtained a wide circulation, was originally composed by the Lord Chief Justice of the Common Pleas, or a Baron of

the Court of Exchequer! Judging merely from a
few isolated facts like these, the strict Churchman
would be too apt to consider the Anglo-Indian
establishment as a sort of hybrid monster, a semi-
military, semi-clerical anomaly, which he could
scarcely bring himself to admit into the member-
ship and communion of the Church of Christ. And
yet, when we calmly consider the real state of things,
we must necessarily be led to a far different conclusion. Let us reflect, that including Ceylon, the
settlements on the coast of Ava, Prince of Wales's
Island, Singapore, and Hong Kong, about one-fifth
of the infantry of the British army, several regiments
of cavalry, and a strong detachment of the Royal
Artillery, are at this time employed in the East.
To these are to be added the East India Company's
civil, military, and medical establishments, and a
large body of European settlers of various descrip-
tions. In enumerating the entire British population,
we must not omit the European ladies and women
of humbler rank ; and probably, it would not be an
over-estimate, if we assume the whole at some 60,000
persons, without counting the numerous Indo-Britons
who are principally located at the several seats of
government. A concise account of the religious
provision which is now made for this numerous
body of our countrymen and their dependants, sepa-
rated from us by many thousand miles of land and
ocean, may not be without its interest to those who,
breaking through the cobwebs of modern philosophy,

" believe in one Catholic and Apostolic Church," and piously " look for the resurrection of the dead, and the life of the world to come."   In contrasting the condition of India, " past and present," in viewing its adaptation to the wants and necessities of a European community, and in enumerating the superior inducements and advantages which it offers to residents in our day, and more particularly to our fair countrywomen, it would be impossible to omit so important an element as the subject which we now propose to consider, cautiously guarding ourselves against polemics, and not having the presumption to touch on doctrinal points, those scholastic subtleties,—

" That cross the proverb, and abound with gall."

It is a topic which will yet require, in order to obtain a clear comprehension of its various bearings, to be treated at some length.

By great perseverance on the part of its early advocates, and by a firm reliance on the blessing of the Author of all good on their pious labours, we have lived to see, as we trust, our national Church, with its ritual and rubrics, firmly planted in British India.

It must not, however, be supposed that its establishment, as we now behold it, was accomplished with as much ease as the usually routine process in our own happy and favoured land. This would afford

a very lame and inadequate idea of the rude and
thorny paths by which, amidst gloom and darkness,
and muttering clouds, the Church was cautiously
conducted through the strait and narrow path, until
she finally emerged into the broad light of day.   At
first she hesitated, and felt oppressed with doubts and
misgivings; she trembled at the difficulties that lay
before her, and recoiled upon herself. But now, "con-
quering and to conquer," undismayed by the sullen
whisperings of infidelity amongst some of her professed adherents, heedless of the deep tones of
the gong from the proud *minar*, and undisturbed
by the thundering of the tom-toms and the shrill
notes of the horns from the temple of Bramah,
she meekly calls together her followers by the joyful
sound of her own Sabbath-bell, and invites them
to assemble within her walls in a strange land, and
by the waters of the Indus and the Ganges, to
tune their harps to the praise and the glory of God.
To form some faint idea of the spiritual condition
of British India in early times, let us suppose a
large town of popular resort, Bath for instance, or
Brighton, without a church or chapel, *except those
of the Church of Rome*, without any observance of
the forms of public worship, except what might be
rarely perhaps, and imperfectly, afforded by the zeal
of some pious layman ; the marriage, baptismal, and
funeral services, performed by a magistrate or a
military officer ; and sometimes the scarcely cold

remains of the once-loved form, hurriedly committed to the unconsecrated ground.

> " No bringing home
> Of bell and burial,
> No requiem and no ceremony else,
> As to peace-parted souls."

With exception, in the one instance, of the population being confined within the circumscribed limits of a town, and in the other widely scattered over an immense continent, in many of the remoter parts of which the European found himself almost in a state of isolation, some notion may be conceived of the unenviable situation in which the Anglo-Indian community were formerly placed.

Even at so recent a period as the commencement of the present century, to many right-thinking persons, and more especially to ladies, with whom, from the superior delicacy of their minds, from an instinctive feeling of dependence, and from the salutary restraints to which they are subjected, an attachment to the mild precepts of our holy religion is almost habitual, the total want of a resident clergyman, excepting at the Presidencies, must have been exceedingly painful. However, notwithstanding the manifold disadvantages under which our countrymen so long laboured, we cannot, without some qualification, admit the sweeping denunciation by the Honourable Mr. Shore, that " the English appear to have considered themselves at liberty to throw aside all considerations of a religious nature;

they lived, indeed, without God in the world, as if there were neither a Heaven nor an *Inferno.*" It will be our business to trace the gradual advancement from this melancholy state of religious destitution, when, as Mr. Shore observes, "shooting, billiards, and all kinds of amusements, are, by the greater part, equally pursued on Sunday as on any other day," to the present far happier condition of India, where there is at least an external observance of the day of rest; and the far greater proportion of the European residents have the option, if they choose to avail themselves of it, of attending divine service once, and in many instances twice, on the Sabbath. We may likewise add that there is no longer a want of adequate provision for the due observance of the other rites and ceremonies of the Church of England, throughout our vast possessions in India.

Amongst the brilliant military exploits that signalised Lord Hardinge's administration, we are too apt to forget the less obtrusive and useful reforms, which, without fussiness or pretence, he quietly and unostentatiously carried out.

"The notification of October 1846," says the *Calcutta Review*, "prohibiting Sunday labour, is evidence of his sincerity, and will be long remembered to his honour. Viewed merely as a secular measure, the good will be great. It will be a check to many, who, having little to do during the week, from mere listlessness or carelessness, were wont to desecrate the sabbath, or permit it to be desecrated by their subordinates. The Moslem and the Hindoo, who worship after their own fashion, have now some proof that the Christian respects the faith he professes."

It cannot excite any surprise that the exemplary Bishop of Calcutta should more particularly allude to this trait in his manly character :—

" Nor can I forget," he writes in a letter, 24th December, 1847, addressed to the Committee of the Inhabitants of Calcutta, "the other services of Lord Hardinge; the honour he has shown to the Christian religion on all occasions, and his prohibition of the continuance of public works on the Lord's day. In fact, Lord Hardinge has crowded into one short administration all the services of the highest order, both military and civil, which have commonly been divided amongst several much larger ones."*

By a notification of June 1846, we find all references to the Post-office prohibited on Sundays; thus affording another proof of the respectful observance of the Christian sabbath.

In contemplating the marked improvement in the social position, and, as we firmly believe, in the rational happiness, of our Anglo-Indian countrymen, there is an adventitious circumstance which may be cursorily alluded to, as it was almost coeval with the re-organisation and large augmentation to the ecclesiastical establishment — we mean the great increase in the number of ladies resorting to the East. In the kindly and genial, yet unassuming

* *Vide* Note 1.

influence, exercised by them over the European society, and in the ready concurrence which they have
always been found to afford to the chaplains in every
work of usefulness, mercy, and benevolence, as well
amongst the poorer classes of their own nation, as
amongst the Indian community, we may mark the
commencement of a new social era. Those who
have paid any attention to the subject are aware,
that on the renewal of the East India Company's
Charter in 1814, after occasioning several protracted
and rather stormy debates in the House of Commons, and a more dignified and temperate discussion
in the Lords, the revised church establishment was
finally settled by Parliament, so far at least as the
principle of an episcopal head was concerned. In
our review of these proceedings we hope not to be
led out of our way by any disrespectful allusions to
the proceedings of the legislature, or by any attempts
to discuss ecclesiastical polity. We are not insensible
to the difficulties to which we are exposed by a strict
adherence to this principle.

The more serious will undervalue our efforts as too
superficial for their graver study; whilst by another
class of readers, from the very nature of our subject,
we shall be censured as too prosy and matter-of-fact
to yield that entertainment they are accustomed
to look for in their desultory reading. We are
conscious that were we to seek to please both
we should assuredly end in being equally unpalatable to either. The graver matter, so far as it

relates to what we may designate as scholastic theology, we willingly resign to critics of a higher calibre: our province it will be to take a popular view of the Anglican Church in its more palpable and immediate effects on the existing relations and on the actual position of Anglo-Indian society, and to mark the favourable contrast which it affords of "the present," as contradistinguished from "the past." Eschewing, then, all those topics, which so often lead to angry disputation, we will confine ourselves to a few such considerations as more appropriately attach to the province of moral theology; we will make it our endeavour to ascertain how far the Church has maintained its character for spiritual efficiency, and been an instrument of good to those under its government. If doctrinal points are studiously avoided, still less would we presume to venture on that *quæstio vexata*, the peculiarities, the properties, and the advantages, which the more zealous members of the Church of England attach to a national state Church. The violent diatribes which of late years have been so continually launched against her, and the serious polemic disputes which have arisen within her own bosom, and which threaten to rend her asunder, and the inquiries that are being made how far she is capable of advantageous adaptation to the altered circumstances of the country, are matters of notoriety to all who take any interest in the proceedings of the day. In the picture which has been sketched of her assailants, by one of her

warmest advocates, we find a sufficient proof that
she has fallen in troubled times. Yet after making
due allowance for the conflicts in which she has
been engaged, and the perils through which she
has passed, the Anglican Church still asserts her
divine origin, and offers herself, to a reasonable
mind, as the best instructor and guide in our
passage through the waves of this troubled world.
That such was the view taken of her by the great
captain of our day we shall presently have occasion to show; and it may be fairly said that whatever may be her faults, her excesses, or her shortcomings, the Church of England has established,
beyond all question, solid and lasting claims on
the gratitude of the country, and has conferred
great blessings on mankind. Whilst her missions
in almost every part of the habitable globe have
contributed to advance the social position of the
natives, to disarm cruelty, and to dispel the darken-
ing gloom of idolatrous superstition, and the horrid
and barbarous rites of paganism, she has, alive to
the progressive spirit of the age, not been idle at
home. Notwithstanding the extravagance of the
claims put forward by a section of her ministers,
more remarkable for zeal than discretion, it cannot
be denied that she has rendered signal service to the
cause of education and morality, and indeed to all
the manifold developements of intellectual and religious life. Her sphere and means of usefulness are
wide and great, and it is much to be lamented that

any portion of her substance, her energy, or her capacity for good, should be wasted in displays of controversial bitterness, or in the more inexcusable follies of protracted strife. When the enemy is at the gate, internal divisions amongst the garrison are the less excusable.

If the justice of these reflections be admitted, it cannot but be considered a providential circumstance that, under the great and good man who now presides over the Church in India, a remarkable spirit of harmony and kindly feeling is generally prevalent amongst the clergy. The importance of this excellent spirit in a land where the national Church is so peculiarly situated, amongst a diversity of races, Christian and heathen, by the more violent of whom she is looked upon with feelings of bitter and undisguised hate, and by the more moderate with covert dislike, can alone be fairly estimated by those who have been residents in the country. So early as 1780, we find the excellent Swartz observing, "The behaviour of the Europeans in this country is truly lamentable;" and although great changes have subsequently taken place in the prevailing cast of thought and sentiment, and India can no longer be reproached as the land of practical infidelity, there is, it is to be feared, enough of the old leaven still remaining to keep the Christian minister continually on the watch. There is every probability that Bishop Heber, whose affections were most tender, and whose heart expanded in good will to all mankind, removed existing prejudices against Christianity, both from European and Indian minds, to a very great extent. It must not, however, be forgotten, that the Church of Rome, which, from a very remote period, planted itself in the heart of Asia, has of late years wonderfully extended the field of its operations. There is scarcely a station, however distant from the seat of Government, where a European regiment is quartered, which is not provided with its chapel and its priests. When to the imposing ceremonies of the Church of Rome—its pageantry, its music, its showy ritual—are superadded Baptists, Independents, Wesleyan Methodists, and Presbyterians, all struggling for precedence, we may form some idea of the obstacles in the way of the Anglican Church.

Being in her nature and principles essentially tolerant, and in that respect most favourably contrasted with the Church of Rome, we are satisfied that the most worthy and enlightened of her members, whilst they hold fast to their own opinions, consider the best safeguard for the preservation of their Church consists in her disposition to deal tenderly with those who dissent from her, and, so far as it is practicable, to live in gentleness, love, and peace, with Christians of all other denominations. Now that we have a parliament composed of men of every variety of creed, the spiritual claims of our distant countrymen, however diversified may be the form of their belief, will be sure to meet with zealous friends and uncompromising advocates in the House of

Commons. The point most to be desired is, that this advocacy may be in some degree guided by local experience, and tempered by sound judgment. It must be remembered that one of the early sources of disquietude to the first Anglican prelate in India, Bishop Middleton, was the controversy in which he found himself involved with the Church of Scotland, the newly-appointed minister of which applied to him for the alternate use of the cathedral in Calcutta, to celebrate divine service according to the Presbyterian form, until a Scotch church was built. We are reminded of this fact by a recent recommendation from the Government of Ceylon, that as

" In the coffee districts the majority of Europeans employed on the estates are Scotsmen and Presbyterians, the places of worship should be jointly used by the ministers of the churches of Scotland and England."

Here is only one instance of the difficulties with which the subject is surrounded, when viewed in connexion with a European population so small in comparison, and so peculiarly situated, as is that of India.

After these preliminary remarks we propose to take a cursory glance, as it affects " India past and present," of the various measures that have at different periods been adopted to supply the spiritual wants of the British population; to provide for the celebration of public worship; and for the adequate performance of these rites and ceremonies which the long-established practice of the Anglican Church has sanctioned and confirmed. We pass over as foreign to our immediate purpose the general state of Christianity in India, which has been so elaborately discussed by the Rev. Mr. Hough, in his valuable work. There is a curious fact related in the Saxon Chronicle, translated by Ingram, that King Alfred, A.D. 883, sent an embassy to India to the shrines of St. Thomas and St. Bartholomew; and we find this embassy also mentioned by Asser, Bishop of Shabara, in his life of King Alfred. We have here, therefore, a confirmation of the great antiquity of the Syrian Church, claiming as its founder St. Thomas the Apostle, which Bishop Heber beautifully described as "having been for ages shedding its lonely and awful light over the woods and mountains of Malabar," and which consisted of about fifty churches principally planted between the mountains and the sea, in the districts extending from Cape Comorin to Cranganore. A considerable portion of these were in communion with the Church of Rome, whose yoke had been forcibly imposed on them by the Portuguese at the close of the sixteenth century; others acknowledged the Patriarch of Antioch: the language in common use amongst them being the Malayalim of the country; and their liturgy and their Scriptures being in the ancient Syriac, to which sacred dialect they adhered with the most scrupulous tenacity. The Armenians, who had always been distinguished for an inflexible adherence to their faith, had erected handsome churches at each of the capitals — Calcutta, Madras, and Bombay, — which were supplied with ministers from Persia, and periodically visited by bishops sent by the Patriarch of Echmiatzin. Although acknowledging seven sacraments, they were not in strict conformity to the Church of Rome, and differed in several respects, both in their worship and their faith, from the Greek and Latin Churches. The sects we have named were, however, but as minnows to the Church of Rome, and more especially to the missions of the Portuguese, which were unrivalled in their zeal, their *dexterity*, and their untiring energy, in planting the religion of the cross in Asia, so that, amidst the ruins into which their temporal possessions have fallen, the vestiges which they have left of their faith, — so calculated by its gorgeous and showy ceremonies to make an impression on the uncultivated mind of the native, — seem destined to survive the *débris* of their earthly grandeur, and to be so firmly rooted that they will never be wholly effaced. According to calculations made some years since by the Abbé Dubois, the congregation of the Church of Rome numbered not less than seven hundred and fifty thousand persons, including as well natives as the descendants of Europeans by alliances with the women of the country; the latter amounting, particularly at the seats of Government of the different Presidencies, to a considerable body, by no means deficient in capacity for business and intelligence; and many of them, by bequest or accumulation,

possessed of wealth. To superintend this large body
of Christians, there were two titular archbishops,
two titular bishops, three vicars apostolic, and a
body of European and native clergy, both secular
and irregular (including several Italian Carmelite
friars), of nearly two thousand individuals. So amply
were the interests of the Romish Church represented
in British India, nor was it in its hierarchy and
priesthood alone that its power was displayed.

" The cathedral of Goa," Dr. Buchanan* described
" as worthy of one of the principal cities of Europe:
whilst it may not inaptly be termed a city of churches:
the magnificence of some of them exceeding any idea I
had formed from previous description: and the wealth
of provinces seems to have been expended in their construction. The church and convent of the Augustins is
a noble pile of building; and the ancient specimens of
architecture at this place far excel anything that has
been attempted in modern times in any other part of
the East."

Bishop Middleton, in his primary visitation, observed that " it is almost impossible to move in any
direction without tracing the footsteps of the Church
of Rome."

The churches of the Roman Catholics at Columba,
we are told, are very grand and gorgeous; and a
modern writer † gives the following description of
the chapel at Trincomalee:—

* Buchanan's " Christian Researches," pp. 155–178.
† Selkirk's " Recollections of Ceylon," p. 370.

" On the outside it is a low, mean-looking building; but in the inside the splendour surpasses anything I could conceive. In the midst of the chapel stood four images, one of the Virgin Mary, another of John the Baptist; I know not whom the others represented."

The account given by the Rev. George Parsons, a very pious and indefatigable missionary, of the place of worship at Monghyr, in Bengal, contrasts rather oddly with this glowing picture :—

" The services are held in a building appropriated to native worship: if I should call it a chapel, I might lead you to form a wrong opinion of it; it consists of mud walls, and an unplastered roof: it is filled with benches, and a small platform, railed round, for a pulpit. To an English eye it looks more like a large barn, seated, than a chapel. But the natives, who are accustomed to mud walls and bare roofs, and who seem to regard a house merely as a shade from the sun, would deem it a very commodious building."

Amidst these gigantic efforts of the Church of Rome, the Protestant nations who held settlements in India had not been altogether idle. When Ceylon was captured by the British army in 1796, the number of native Protestant Christians " was stated to be about 340,000, divided by the Dutch into 240 church-ships or parishes, in each of which one Protestant school was erected, and attached to the church. A seminary was likewise established for the instruction of native youths of promising abilities in the Dutch language, as a medium for the acquisition of knowledge, which might qualify them for the office of catechists, or of preachers, among their own country-men."

The Danish mission, established under two most exemplary missionaries, Ziegenbalg and Plutscth, at Tranquebar, made considerable progress, and in 1787 appears to have numbered, partly of natives, partly descendants of natives and Europeans, nearly 18,000 persons. About the year 1710, the Society for Pro-moting Christian Knowledge, (towards the furthering and extending of which Bishop Middleton incessantly laboured,) turned its attention to India; and shortly after Mr. Stevenson, the chaplain at Madras, formed a native school there, and in 1729 the congregation amounted to about 140. This was followed by another mission at Cuddalore, near the French capital of Pondicherry, where, in 1767, a church was erected; and in 1774, another establishment was formed at Negapatam, on that seaport being captured from the Dutch. The celebrated Swartz founded the Trichinopoly mission, which in 1817 appears to have numbered about 460; and on Bishop Middleton's first visit to the south of India, the number of native Protestant Christians attached to the Protestant Epi-scopal communion was calculated at somewhere about 23,000. The small remnant of the Jewish tribes widely scattered over the land, and known by the distinguishing appellations of White and Black Jews, the latter dating their emigration about A.C. 508, may be reckoned at 10,000. Other Protestant institutions, amongst the most active of which was the London Baptist Society settled at Serampore near Calcutta, were likewise labouring with great zeal, but, it is feared, with comparatively little success, in the propagation of Christianity, according to Protestant forms, in Hindoostan. When compared with the magnificence with which the Roman Catholic rites were celebrated at Goa, *where the Inquisition reared its fearful front,* the less showy and more simple forms of the Calvinistic and other sects appear comparatively insignificant. Still, such as they were, they called forth those memorable words of Bishop Heber, " Here is the strength of the Christian cause in India."

We are indebted for the condensed summary we have presented to a very valuable work, Le Bas's " Life of Bishop Middleton," and to the " Letters of the Abbé Dubois."

In the early part of the seventeenth century, when our commercial relations with the East had greatly extended, and when, for the reception of that body which has. ever since retained the immediate government of our vast territories, the East India House was built, there are some few indications that the labours of the missionaries, in the absence of any regular clergy, were not altogether overlooked. The vigorous mind of George the First, a man of more than moderate talent, appears to have been attracted to the subject; whilst his well-known and marked distrust of those who were suspected of High-

Church principles, would the more readily incline him to look with favour on Ziegenbalg, Grendlerus, and other pious men, who were working in this distant vineyard. But the most influential amongst those who sought to advance the mild doctrines of the Protestant faith, was a very eminent prelate, Dr. Wake, archbishop of Canterbury, many of whose letters to the missionaries in India remain on record, and evince the lively interest he took in the furtherance of Christianity.

But until the commencement of the present century, notwithstanding the giant steps with which the British power advanced from a few insignificant factories, dedicated to commercial purposes, to an enormous and majestic empire, little, indeed, appears to have been attempted for enlightening the natives, who became gradually subjected to our sway. Here and there a few enthusiasts were to be found who strenuously advocated conversion — sometimes, it is to be feared, after the manner of the " intelligent boy " mentioned by Layard in his " Nineveh : "—

" Young as he might be, he was already a precocious pupil of Shaeik Tabor; and when I put him upon a religious topic, he entered most gravely into an argument to prove the obligations imposed upon Mussúlmen to exterminate the unbelievers, supporting his theological views by very apt quotations from the Koran."

In preferring " this rough-and-ready method " of enforcing the doctrines of Christianity, these worthy zealots would seem to have altogether lost sight of the only practical method by which they could hope to carry their project to a successful result. The faggot and the sword have ever been found but indifferent weapons, when the appeal ought rather to be made to reason. Information gained through the medium of education, is the far safer armour to be used in opposing idolatry and superstition. By softening the passions, and shedding its mild influence over the mind, and by lifting the veil which conceals the horrid sacrifices of Moloch, or the detestable worship of Brahma, it will gradually awaken, without alarming, the more intelligent natives to a sense of their benighted condition.

It must, however, in justice be admitted, that for the space of about a century from the granting of the charter to the East India Company by William the Third in 1698, to its successive renewals up to 1793, the legislature never totally lost sight of the moral and religious welfare of India, and of the responsibilities which it had incurred. But the views of Parliament seem to have been confined within a narrow sphere, and to have been satisfied with a resolution passed in 1793, and which could apply only to the then limited European residents, "That sufficient means of religious worship and instruction be provided for all persons of the Protestant communion in the service, or under the protection, of the East India Company in Asia, proper ministers being from time to time sent out from Great Britain for those purposes."

During the period we have been considering, it is evident that the attention paid to the progress of ecclesiastical matters in India, and to the upholding of our holy religion, was partial, confined, and cursory. But shortly previous to the granting of the Company's charter in 1814, we enter upon a new era, distinguished by a marked change, not only abroad but at home.

All the early writers on India who have noticed the Church establishment, agree in its total inadequacy to supply even the wants of the European population, and still more in its comparative insignificance, when " elbowed" by the Romish churches at Goa and other places, and by those stupendous memorials of a gigantic superstition, which the pagodas and the mosques of the natives everywhere exhibited. There cannot be a more melancholy picture than that given by the Hon. Mr. Shore, in his very able " Notes on Indian Affairs," of the dearth of clergymen, and the consequences that naturally resulted from this gap in our colonial arrangements. Mr. Forbes tells us that during his residence in India, there were seldom more than two chaplains for the Presidency of Bombay, one being permanently stationed at the seat of Government, and the other alternately between Surat and Baroche. He says, though the case appears to have been by no means an exceptional one, that whilst stationed in Guzerat he " felt, for nearly four years together, a privation of all the sacred ordinances of Christianity and at-

tendance at public worship ;" and he complains that
whilst the Roman Catholic missionaries were actively
labouring in their vocation, " the higher classes of
European society continue in thoughtless indolence,
lukewarmness, or infidelity, and the garrisons and
cantonments are left without any religious in-
structors." He was particularly struck by a native,
in his own artless, expressive style, asking him this
important question, " You call yourselves Christians,
so do the Roman Catholics, *who abound in India ;*
they daily frequent their churches, fast and pray,
and use many penances. The English alone appear
unconcerned about an event of the greatest importance."*

Lord Valentia in his " Travels,"† has the following
observations :—

" It will hardly be believed that in the splendid city
of Calcutta there is only one church of the Establishment, and that by no means conspicuous either for size
or ornament."

He says, further, remarking on the peculiar tempt-
ations to which the freedom of manners exposes the
clergy :—

" It is painful to observe that the characters of some
of that order are by no means creditable to the doctrines
they profess. In every point of view, *political* as well as
religious, it is highly desirable that men of liberal edu-

* *Vide* Note 2. † Vol. i. p. 246.

cation and exemplary piety should be employed; who by their manners would improve the tone of society in which they lived, and by the sacredness of their character operate as a check on the tendency to licentiousness that too frequently prevails. The native inhabitants of Calcutta may, from the sight of the one solitary church, believe that we have a national religion, but I know of nothing that can give this information to our distant Eastern subjects."

We find a passage in a letter from the venerable Swartz, in 1769, "What you write touching the clergyman is doleful indeed;" which bears witness to the want of caution exhibited in those days in the selection of chaplains. But even when there were chaplains, it appears that their services were not always required; for we find it stated in the " Memoirs of Dr. Buchanan," on his appointment to the cantonment of Barrackpore,—

"The station at that period possessed no place for public worship, and divine service was never required by the military staff to which he was attached."

Dr. Buchanan, in one of his letters to Mr. Charles Grant, written about a twelvemonth afterwards, says :—

"Lord Mornington has been at Barrackpore for ten days past; he was surprised when I told him that we never had divine service there, or at any other station. He was still more surprised when he heard there were horse-races here on Sunday morning." *

* Pearson's " Memoirs of Buchanan," vol. i. p. 161.

Fervent as was the zeal, earnest as were the efforts, persevering as were the labours of the great body of the clergy at home, and more particularly of those who were connected with the Society for the Promotion of Christian Knowledge, they were effectually seconded by the instrumentality of laymen in their great undertaking. It was impossible to meet with a more energetic and strenuous advocate than was Wilberforce, in endeavouring to work on the higher classes of society, and in seeking to convince them of the efficacy of that faith to which he had so warmly attached himself. But even he was surpassed by a fellow-labourer, the celebrated Mrs. Hannah More; who, after having been the familiar friend and guest of Garrick, and having, under his auspices, successfully cultivated dramatic literature, devoted herself at a later period of her life, with equal ardour, to the advancement of those great truths, with the importance of which she had become deeply impressed. Dissenting in some degree from the views which we are sure were conscientiously entertained, and were most forcibly expressed in the voluminous writings of these two celebrated authors, we are compelled to acknowledge the great talent which they brought into the field, and the genuine proofs of sincerity and strong conviction by which they were evidently actuated. Verging, in some slight degree, towards puritanism, they were, nevertheless, amongst those to whom it was least indebted; for by rousing the Church from the apathy in which it had, it is to be feared, too much indulged, and in awakening it to the peril by which it was environed, they acted like skilful surgeons, who to save the patient probe the wound to the quick. Thus the zeal and enthusiasm with which the different denominations of Dissenters laboured — more especially in Wales, and in some of the great seats of our manufactures — to obtain proselytes, were now met by countervailing exertions on the part of a very large proportion of the Anglican Church to retain their flocks in their proper fold. By this powerful and energetic body no endeavours were omitted to widen the sphere of her influence, to draw more closely into her fold the hesitating and the lukewarm, and to win back those who had strayed from her sacred precincts into the turbid waters of dissent. The works of Mrs. Hannah More penetrated even into the cold regions of fashion; and in spite of the shrug, the smile, and the sneer, there is reason to believe that many a *fair* convert was made to doctrines which proscribed the opera, the ball-room, the race-course, and the other *agrémens* of gaiety and opulence, and substituted for them the milder and less exciting pleasures of the domestic hearth. The earnest appeals of Wilberforce, likewise directly aimed at the pomps and the vanities of the world, and at the nothingness of their conclusions, obtained a most extensive circulation; and aided by the personal exertions of the clergy, many of the middle and upper classes, who did not actually go the whole length of the author's views, yet accompanied him to a certain point, and gave a general adherence to the correctness of the principles which he strove to inculcate.

Still the line taken by Mr. Wilberforce, and adopted by others who wrote in the same spirit, in dividing society, more especially the higher and middle classes, into the rather offensive distinction of *real* and nominal Christians, could not be expected to be quietly assented to. In his own case it was somewhat softened by the exemplary tenor of his life, by his benevolence and extensive charity, by the simplicity of his character, by his unquestioned and unquestionable sincerity, and, perhaps more than all, by the *prestige* that attached to his noble position, as one of the most eloquent and eminent advocates for the abolition of the slave-trade, which terminated in an immortal triumph of Christianity and civilisation over stolid selfishness and brutal barbarism. There were those, however, neither few in number, nor insignificant in station, who, whilst they accorded to the steady, consistent, and uncompromising champion of morality, virtue, and religion, a certain degree of praise, which no occasional want of judgment, or intemperance of zeal on his part, could altogether extinguish, would not extend the same degree of forbearance to others amongst his disciples and followers. It was considered no small presumption in these persons to arrogate to themselves exclusively the name and designation of Christians. Nor is it

to be wondered at, if in the fashionable world many
were to be found who could reconcile to their own
consciences a proper sense of religion and of their
relative duties to man and God, although they de-
murred from an absolute sequestration from public
amusements of a more refined and intellectual description, as well as a participation in the gaieties,
perhaps it would not be using too strong a term to
say — the frivolities of fashion.   Now by the *real*
— as they designated themselves — Christians, all
who came under this category were set down as
nominal Christians; whilst the latter, in retaliation,
lampooned and ridiculed the former as " righteous
overmuch."   We think it but fair to conclude that
the shafts of their satire were mainly directed against
those who, like the Pharisee, held themselves up as
holier than their neighbours, whose religion was so
strongly tinctured with vanity, as to lead to the
ostentatious and unreasonable pretensions of a superior degree of sanctity, which general society was
indisposed to admit.   We cannot bring ourselves to
believe that it was ever intended to pronounce a con-
demnation of sterling goodness, and high moral principle, when these were found in the unassuming
garb of modesty, united with consistency of conduct.
In short, the reproof was intended for those who,
violating the tacit compact of society, and affecting a
sort of stilted superiority, made themselves morose,
unsocial, and *disagreeable;* and justly exposed themselves and their pretences to the calm rebuke of the

more moderate, and to the stinging lash of the satirist. That we are not altogether wrong in our conclusions, we think we have a memorable instance in the *Joan of Arc* of the party, Mrs. Hannah More. Although this lady had, in her youthful days, been on familiar terms with many of the wits and celebrities of the day—persons whose range of moral duties, however brilliant their talents, fell very far beneath that severe and rigid code which the *real* Christians set up as the test of orthodoxy; we do not find that, in so total a change of opinion, her motives were impugned, or her sincerity questioned.

It would be invidious to contrast the aristocratic character of the prelates of a former period, many of them nobly descended, with the more energetic, if less highly connected, episcopal bench of our day. Nor would we have even incidentally alluded to it, but for one circumstance. Although there were thousands of European soldiers in the King's and Company's service, dispersed in the various stations in India, whose spiritual interests, except at the Presidencies, were almost totally unprovided for, notwithstanding an agreement had been entered into by the East India Company to maintain a sufficient number of chaplains for the purpose, it does not appear that any remonstrance proceeded from the right reverend bench on the neglect in carrying out this solemn compact. Such complaints would probably have been unpalatable to the Government of the day, and it would therefore perhaps be unfair to have expected that Churchmen, much engrossed with the turmoils and contests that were agitating the mother country, should have gone out of their way to point out the awful spiritual destitution in which their exiled countrymen were involved. Good and amiable as was the Marquis Cornwallis, and sincerely anxious as he was to advance the interests of the officers of the Company's service, and to secure to them the possession of those great privileges, from which they had for so long a period been debarred, it would not appear that the almost total deficiency of chaplains, and the impossibility of observing the Sabbath at the great Mofussil stations of the army, which were the head-quarters of European regiments, occupied his attention, or found a place in those extensive and liberal regulations which were carried into effect in January 1796. It is singular that so truly excellent a man should have so totally overlooked this most important point in connexion with the improvements which were introduced into the army.

" Does it not appear a proper thing to wise and good men in England," says Dr. Buchanan, "(for after a long residence in India we sometimes lose sight of what is accounted proper at home), does it not seem proper, *when a thousand British soldiers are assembled at a remote station in the heart of Asia, that the Sabbath of their country should be noticed?* That, at least, it should not become what it is, and ever must be, where there is no religious restraint, a day of peculiar profligacy? To us it would appear not only a politic, but a *humane*

act, in respect of these our countrymen,, to hallow
the seventh day. Of a thousand soldiers in sickly India
there will, generally speaking, be a hundred who are in
a declining state of health—who, after a long struggle
with the climate *and with intemperance*, have fallen into
a dejected and hopeless state of mind, and pass their
time in painful reflection on their distant homes, their
absent families, and on the indiscretions of past life—
but whose hearts would revive within them on their
entering once more the house of God, and hearing the
absolution of the Gospel to the returning sinner.

" The oblivion of the Sabbath in India is that which
properly constitutes *banishment* from our country. The
chief evil of our exile is found here; for this extinction
of the sacred day tends, more than anything else, to
eradicate from our minds respect for the religion and
affection for the manners and institutions, and even for
the local scenes, of early life."*

The example of George the Third and his Queen
was not without its influence at court; and, generally speaking, amongst the higher circles there
might be remarked a more sober observance of
the Sabbath, an abstinence from any open dese-
cration of this hallowed day, and in other respects
a more decorous and habitual conformity with the
obvious precepts of morality, which, if they did
not count for great things in the opinion of the
more serious, at least formed a striking contrast

* Buchanan's " Memoir on an Ecclesiastical Establishment
for India," p. 18.

with that indifference with which it had been cus-
tomary to treat everything of a sacred nature.

Independent of the untiring and never-to-be-
forgotten exertions of many of the most zealous
and the most talented of the clergy, there were
other causes at work which lent a powerful aid to
their pious labours. The disorders by which France
had for many years been convulsed, the atrocities
that marked the reign of terror, and the fearful
bouleversement by which the throne was shivered
and the *noblesse* and the priesthood scattered to the
winds, caused the strongest minds to pause, and
even to tremble for the future. At a subsequent
stage of the Revolution, when the Goddess of Reason
was substituted for the Great I AM — when semi-
pagan observances and unhallowed orgies supplanted
the worship, even in a corrupt form, of the living
Jehovah — when

> " Those, the fiends who near ally'd,
> O'er Nature's wounds and wrecks preside"—

and when the streets of Paris and other great cities
were deluged with blood,—Europe looked on aghast,
and in awful suspense awaited the issue.

Contemptible as the *Age of Reason* may now
appear to us, and forgotten as have long been the
swelling periods of Burke, the lesson was not lost
upon the sober-minded people of England. States-
men, hitherto, perhaps, like Gallio, " caring for
none of those things" that pertained to religion, or

viewing it, after the courtly fashion of Lord Chester-
field, "as a respectable and conservative institution,"
were perforce compelled to acknowledge its importance when they witnessed the astounding results of
the triumph of the French Encyclopedists. It was
a wily, and perhaps we may admit, considering the
agitated state of society in those troublous times, a
politic artifice, to connect disloyalty in some degree
with dissent. Unfortunately there were those amongst
the most eminent of the Nonconformist divines who
gave some colour for this reproach by employing
language of the most inflammatory kind, and, considering the threatening aspect of the political horizon, by using threats of no ambiguous import against
those who firmly adhered to "Church and King."
It followed that, by their own indiscretion, the fetters
were still more closely riveted, and more difficulties
were thrown in the way of that toleration which, at
the risk of displeasing some of our readers, we must
consider to be the glory of the present times. Fortunately those stormy days are long past, and, unless
in some of the recent sallies of Young Ireland, the
present generation lives in blissful ignorance of the
intense bitterness and the deep-rooted animosity
with which the controversy between Churchman and
Dissenter was formerly carried on. Yet, even to the
present hour, one great political party, which to a
certain extent allied itself with dissent, has never
been able entirely to shake off the imputation, if not
of actual hostility, at least of want of sympathy with

the Established Church." Thus fully occupied with
more immediate interests at home, the indifference
with which India was viewed, until the public mind
was suddenly roused into action by causes which
we shall proceed to explain, will scarcely occasion
surprise.

Such, we believe, we are justified in considering to
have been the general tone and feeling of society in
the higher and middle classes of Great Britain, as it
related to serious matters, about the period of which
we have been treating. To this, however, there was
an exception. The great party which, under the
guidance of Wilberforce, Thornton, and other names,
if of less celebrity, certainly not of less zeal, gradually developed itself, became commonly known as
the religious world, and was destined to play a principal part in the national drama. We have dwelt at
greater length than we should otherwise have done
on the state of opinion at home, as it is intimately
connected with the extraordinary change which took
place in those interests which attach to the more
immediate subject of our inquiry. The immense
distance of India, and the slowness of communication
between Great Britain and the East, naturally pro-
duced an indifference and apathy, which, amidst the
distractions and convulsions of the European world,
required some startling event, such as the victories
of Clive or the trial of Warren Hastings, to dispel.
Under the most discouraging circumstances, however, the Society for Promoting Christian Knowledge

had, from an early period, endeavoured, though in a
limited way, to uphold the great cause of Christianity, and now, stimulated by *the religious world*
into a more decided course of action, placed themselves in the van in those strong appeals to the
Legislature which were shortly to produce such
important results. But the Society, however influential from its connexion with the highest dignita-
ries of the Anglican Church, did not stand alone in
its efforts to rouse a national feeling in favour of the
cause which it had taken up. The Rev. Claudius
Buchanan, one of the ablest men who was at that
time attached to the Church in India as a military
chaplain, and who had for some time, under the auspices and to the entire satisfaction of the Marquis of
Wellesley, filled the important office of Vice-Provost
of the College of Fort William, entered heart and soul
into the cause. His clear and lucid arguments, and
his powerful pleas in favour of an effective episcopacy
for India, gained additional credit with the public
from his local experience, derived from a residence
of several years in Bengal, and which enabled him in
his " *Christian Researches,*" and other valuable pub-
lications, to state explicitly and plainly the spiritual
wants of the country. Naturally of a bold and
ardent temperament, habitually generous, possessed
of fine abilities united to great command of temper,
perspicuous and decisive in his writings, not exclusively Calvinistic, but embracing, it is believed, the
doctrine of divine predestination, which must have

nerved his strong mind for its work, it may readily
be supposed that the labours of such a man would
be invaluable, and would tell with powerful effect in
the long and arduous contest that was about to com-
mence between the advocates and the opponents of
the important measures that were proposed for the
advancement of Christianity in the East. The two
grand objects at which he aimed were, in the first
instance, such an enlarged ecclesiastical establishment as would provide for the requirements of the
Anglo-Indian inhabitants, amounting, perhaps, in
round numbers, to between 38,000 and 40,000, and
spread over an immense breadth of country, from
Delhi to Cape Comorin, and from the frontiers of
Nepaul to Bombay. The second and more questionable point was to obtain the sanction of the
Legislature for the employment of missionaries by
the various religious societies, who were anxious to
improve the religious and moral state of the benighted native population. The policy of the first
of these objects found more favour, and was more
generally admitted when it became a substantive
proposition for discussion in the House of Commons, than it experienced in other quarters. Although the religious world had penetrated into
Leadenhall Street, and was represented by two or
three of the most influential directors, there would
appear to have been a strong feeling on the part of
the majority against so large an augmentation, involving an episcopacy, as was proposed. Nor was

the heavy addition that would be made to the previous burdens which the revenue had to sustain, and
which had recently been added to by a greatly increased civil and military establishment, lost sight
of by the opponents of the measure. One can
scarcely wonder that these prudential considerations
should outweigh others of a less mundane nature,
when it is remembered that the proposition involved in its consequences no slight addition to the
demands on an exchequer which, with the innumerable parings and clippings of later years, had, at
Madras and Bombay, never come up to the ex-
penditure; and which was solely indebted to the
rich and well-administered provinces under the Presidency of Bengal, for making up the deficiency.
These, however, resolved themselves into fiscal considerations, and were but of secondary importance,
in comparison with the very great degree of in-
quietude and alarm which was occasioned by the
open manifestation of a design for an extensive
attempt at the conversion of the natives, to be
made through the instrumentality of missionaries.
It was here that the cloud gathered in its gloomiest
aspect; and there were recent circumstances connected with the history of India which threw a dark
shadow over the sunny projects of the inexperienced
and the sanguine. But a few years had elapsed since
the whole of Southern India was astounded by a
formidable mutiny of the native soldiery, who gar-
risoned the strong fortress of Vellore, and which

led to a dreadful and indiscriminate massacre of European officers and soldiers, and occasioned the most alarming suspicions of the degree of confidence to be reposed in the native army, whose fidelity and attachment no reverses of fortune had hitherto been enabled to shake. It was considered by many at the time, although we have every reason to believe erroneously, to have originated in a dread on the part of the native population, of a covert design to compel them by physical force to abandon their religion, and to embrace the tenets of Christianity.

As is usual on similar occasions, the press teemed with pamphlets, putting forward the views of the advocates and opponents of the proposed changes; and in one of the latter, purporting to be written by a field-officer at Madras, and published by Cadell and Davies in 1813, we read the following almost incredible piece of folly :—

"In one instance, military authority had been employed at Ceylon *to compel the Sepoys to frequent our church;* and on different occasions the conduct of the missionaries in the interior provinces had been at variance with the civil, judicial, and military authorities of the Government."

It must be allowed, that, independent of its own absurdity, the fact, being given on anonymous authority, is not in favour of its authenticity. Still, statements of such a nature could not fail to exert

some influence ; and no wonder that even cool and
reflecting men viewed with a sensitiveness, which,
in our day may appear exaggerated, the advent of
any legislative enactments, which might by possibility lead to a renewal of the perilous position in
which the Presidency of Madras had been so recently placed. In recording the history of these
transactions, it is necessary that this important fact
should be prominently placed in view, in order satis-
factorily to account for what might otherwise appear
the intemperate conduct and extreme violence of
the opposition. The Society for Promoting Christian Knowledge, aided by the wide-spread influence
of the religious world, had not been remiss in their
labours during the recess; and accordingly on the
assembling of Parliament in 1813, the tables of both
houses groaned under the weight of innumerable
petitions, demanding the interference of the Legislature in behalf of the moral and religious interests
of India. We advisedly avail ourselves of the word
" *demanding,*" instead of requesting, as from the intemperate tone in which some of these addresses were
couched, they authorise the use of the stronger term.
Upwards of nine hundred addresses, several of them
most numerously signed, were obtained from the
cities, towns, and even, in some instances, from
many of the inconsiderable villages of the United
Kingdom. In some of these the more unreflecting
partisans of the movement evinced, by their florid
language, that they actually contemplated the insane

project of turning the British possessions in India into a second Mexico; and following the example which had been originally set by the Portuguese at Goa, in their high and palmy days, they desired not to trust altogether to the milder weapons of reason and argument in order to carry out their favourite theory of conversion. That Wilberforce, Stephen, W. Smith, and the leaders of the party, took more sober and statesmanlike views, and that they were in some measure disconcerted by the folly and violence of the more injudicious of their followers, are matters of history. Still they were persons not of a nature to be daunted by difficulties in pursuing what they considered a just and righteous cause; and the more formidable the obstacles appeared to be (some of them interposed by the blind infatuation of their own partisans), the more eager and indefatigable were their efforts to overcome them. The sagacity of Mr. Wilberforce clearly perceived the dilemma in which he was placed; and it is but doing him bare justice to say that it roused him to efforts fully worthy of the righteous cause he had undertaken. He saw at a glance, that the arguments with which he had to contend would, if they succeeded in obtaining the ear of the House, not stop at the prevention of conversion only, but, if allowed their full sway, would have likewise demolished altogether the project of an episcopal establishment. He knew it had been boldly asserted that the party who now occupied so prominent a position were not disposed

to stick at trifles; and that if not prepared to go the
length of Mahomet in the East, and the Jesuits in
South America, they yet contemplated drawing the
entire native population within the pale of Christianity, by other and more forcible methods than those of
argument and reason. The assailants, who saw the
most vulnerable point, brought all their force to
bear upon it; and two members of the House of
Commons, Sir Henry Montgomery and Mr. Lushington, who possessed the advantage of a practical
knowledge of the subject from residence in India,
were amongst the most conspicuous, both in perti-
nacity and in vehemence. It was to overthrow their
statements, therefore, that Mr. Wilberforce particularly directed himself; and his speeches, in several
debates of unusual length and interest, were acknowledged, even by opponents, to be masterpieces of
oratory, such as St. Stephen's had seldom witnessed
of late years. It is, perhaps, not too much to say,
that to the fervour of his language, to the purity
and elegance of his style, and to the strain of impassioned and irresistible eloquence with which he
bore down all opponents, the ultimate success of the
cause was mainly to be attributed. Fully alive to
the alarm which had been excited, even amongst
many temperate and impartial persons, by the measures proposed for the introduction of Christianity,
according to the Protestant form, which had only as
yet obtained a footing in some parts of Southern
India, he took care to be most explicit on this point:

" But let it never be forgotten, it is *toleration* only that we seek ; *we utterly disclaim all ideas of proceeding by methods of compulsion or authority.* Compulsion and Christianity ! why, the terms are at variance with each other ; the ideas are incompatible. In the language of inspiration itself, Christianity has been called ' the law of liberty.' "

In a masterly speech, delivered on 22d June, 1813, he expressed his " dissent from the opinion that it might be advisable to employ our regular clergy as missionaries." This drew on him, in a subsequent warm debate, the cutting retort,—

" The Church of England it appears, then, is to send out no missionaries at all. She is to be provided, in-deed, with her bishops and her archdeacons, and is to loll in dignified ease upon her episcopal cushions. But the supporters of the clause have reserved all their pious zeal for the missionaries." *

As to the professed purpose for which these mis-sionaries were to be sent out, it was further re-marked :—

" An honourable gentleman has said, that petitions for that object had been received from all parts of the coun-try. But it should also be stated that they uniformly came from the same description of people, *who even went further than the resolutions of the House, for it seems now that nothing less than the total conversion of the Hindoos could satisfy their zeal.*" †

* Mr. Lushington's speech : Hansard, vol. xxvi. p. 1019.
† Hansard, vol. xxvi. p. 562.

From the few brief extracts we have given of the parliamentary proceedings in 1813, the difficulties with which the religious world had to contend, and the perseverance with which they were encountered, will be clearly perceived. Although public opinion was not brought to bear on the question with that irresistible force, and with that almost perfect unanimity, with which we have seen it recently exhibited on occasion of filling up one of the highest appointments in India, still there was somewhat of an inconvenient pressure from without, to aid the zeal of the party within the House. Although introduced by the ministry, and supported by the. whole force of the Government, who, on ordinary occasions, could command a sweeping majority, it was not till after the most strenuous opposition, and after vehement and acrimonious discussion, that they were enabled to pass in committee of the whole House, on the 12th July, 1813, two resolutions,* the former of which (the twelfth) hereto subjoined, was much less keenly contested than the latter (the thirteenth), which, relating to the missionaries, is foreign to our immediate subject :—

"That it is the opinion of this committee, that it is expedient that the Church establishment in the British territories in the East Indies should be placed under the superintendence of a bishop and three archdeacons,

* Hansard, vol. xxvi. p. 1207.

and that adequate provision should be made from the territorial revenues of India for their maintenance."

This resolution, being subsequently made the foundation of a corresponding clause in the bill — the cause which had excited so much interest in the religious world, and for some time occasioned such intense anxiety—was to a certain extent triumphant, in spite of all opposition. Though it fell short of their ardent expectations, and was considered by them clearly inadequate to the spiritual exigencies of a territory which stretched over no less than twenty degrees of latitude and ten degrees of longitude—from Delhi to Cape Comorin, and from the Indus to the Ganges—they had the satisfaction of not only seeing the Church solemnly recognised, but, like all the other departments of the service in India, placed under the efficient control and superintendence of an immediate superior. The Act which renewed the charter of the Company erected their territories into one vast diocese, with three archdeacons, of which one was to be resident at each of the Presidencies. The salary of the bishop was fixed at 5000l. a-year, and of the archdeacons at 2000l.; and although, in European estimation, these salaries would appear abundantly liberal, they must be viewed in connexion with the necessarily expensive establishments required by the climate, and by the general mode of living which custom has recognised in the East among persons of high rank and station.

And here we may, not inappropriately, record a noble instance of munificence, unexampled in our day, on the part of the venerable prelate who now fills the episcopal throne. For years he has devoted a large portion of his salary — not less, if we are correctly informed, than 20,000*l.* — to the erection of a magnificent cathedral in the metropolis of British India.

Lord Valentia, as we have seen, mentions it as a reproach to "the splendid city of Calcutta," that it possessed only "one church of *the Establishment,* and that by no means conspicuous either for size or ornament."* This blot on the capital of India no longer exists ; for, in addition to eight churches of the Establishment, the noble structure commenced by Bishop Wilson is fast approaching to completion, and, like the college founded by Bishop Middleton, will form a splendid ornament to "the city of palaces," and be for ever associated with an affectionate remembrance of one of the most exemplary and the most distinguished of our Indian prelates.

The wedge having thus been inserted, and the first step gained, much anxiety was naturally felt as to the person to be nominated to a charge, not only startling from its novelty, and from the ominous ill-bodings of those opposed to episcopacy, but appalling from its gigantic magnitude, from the peculiar

* "Voyages and Travels of Viscount Valentia," vol. i. p. 243. For an excellent account of the cathedral, see the "British Friend of India Magazine," vol. ii. p. 157.

E

difficulties which local circumstances offered to its
due developement, and from the disadvantages which
a tropical climate would present to a man who must,
in the ordinary nature of things, have passed the
meridian of life. When it became known, however,
that the choice had fallen on Archdeacon Middleton,
vicar of the populous parish of St. Pancras, favourably known to the learned world by his admirable
treatise on the doctrine of the Greek article, and not
less conspicuous for those unwearied efforts which
have been so worthily followed up by the present
vicar, Mr. Dale, to advance the spiritual and temporal
interests of that great metropolitan parish, it occasioned, if not universal, yet almost general satisfaction. Looking back, after an interval of nearly forty
years, and with the light which the very valuable
memoir of the Rev. Mr. Le Bas has afforded us, it
seems scarcely possible to have made a more judicious choice of the prelate who was destined to be
the father and founder of the Protestant Episcopal
Church of our Asiatic empire. Tall and commanding
in his person, with a finely-proportioned form, that
indicated both activity and vigour, with an intelligent
countenance, and features regular and handsome, he
was the *beau idéal* of the dignified ecclesiastic, so far
as external appearances can convey that impression.
Nor were these natural advantages belied by any
shortcomings of the inner man. Although of a
sanguine temperament, he was at times liable to a
depression of spirits, to which the debilitating effects

of the climate would materially conduce, but which
he appears to have effectually struggled against with
all the energies of his strong and powerful mind.
Full of zeal and of indomitable perseverance in the
pursuit of objects which his conscience told him
were praiseworthy — neglecting nothing, even to the
minutest details, which he considered essential to the
welfare of his immense diocese—he was possessed of
that rare and excellent judgment, of that nice per-
ception, of that habitual prudence and caution, that
enabled him to bear up against the discouraging
effects of unreasonable and sometimes vexatious
opposition. Of his capacity as a practical man of
business, his intimate connexion during many years
with the Society for Promoting Christian Knowledge
had afforded abundant proof. Distinguished as a
fine classical scholar, his editorship of the "British
Critic" had earned for him the meed of well-merited
praise, as a sound and orthodox divine. His early
habits of self-control, tempered and corrected some
little tendency to nervous excitement, which he occasionally displayed, and which appears, except in rare
instances, to be the usual concomitant of superior
minds. Ardent in the acquisition of knowledge,
more especially of such a nature as could be made
conducive to the welfare of the Church in India,
which was evinced by his laborious study of the
history of the Syriac Churches, and of those other
legacies of remote antiquity to the cause of Christianity which he discovered in his extensive tours, he

was never unemployed; and yet, with that modesty which, though not obtrusively paraded, formed a pleasing element in his character, he writes to a friend in England,—

"I am quite surprised at the little I get through, but I am always at work, and as full of projects as ever."

Much has been written as to the neglect and indifference to religion that generally prevailed in the European community; and Dr. Buchanan gives a very striking instance of the great evil that resulted from there being no regular head of the Church to superintend and regulate all matters appertaining to its ordinances :—

"Before Lord Teignmouth left India, Mr. Brown procured an order in council that the military in the garrison should attend at the Presidency Church every Sunday morning at six o'clock, there being no chapel for service in the garrison itself. Strong opposition was made to this order, on the ground that the troops would suffer in their health by marching in the sun. They attended a few Sundays; but at last the clamour became so violent that the order was revoked, and the triumph over religion rendered complete."

He adds, however, that when he was in Calcutta on a Sunday, he usually performed service at the hospital, where, though there was no regular audience, "there was always a succession of hearers."

In another letter he says :—

"Infidelity raged here with great violence formerly,

but it is rather on the *defensive* now. It was fashionable
to allege that Oriental research was not favourable to
the truth of Christianity, but the contrary is found to be
the case. I am constantly applied to by families, religious, moral, and dissipated, to name books for them,
and I do what I can."

We find a notice in Dr. Carey's Journal of 24th
January, 1794, subsequently so well known as one
of the most faithful and zealous missionaries in
Bengal :—

" This morning went to visit a professor of religion
to whom I was recommended, at the Isle of Wight, but,
to my sorrow, found him at dice."

We may easily conjecture the surprise of this
worthy minister at the worldly amusement by which
he found his friend's mornings were occupied.

But free-thinking was not confined to Bengal,
for we find the simple-minded Forbes,* whose gentle
nature shrunk from "setting down aught in malice,"
compelled to bear reluctant testimony to a similar
state of opinion in Bombay :—

" I have been asked by many natives of India whether
we really believed the truths of our own Scriptures, when
our general conduct so little corresponded with their
divine injunctions. What may now be the prevailing
practice I cannot say : certainly the spirit of Christianity

* "Oriental Memoirs," vol. iii. p. 56.

was not then the actuating principle of European society in India. A thoughtlessness of futurity, a carelessness about religious concerns, were more prominent. Highly as I esteemed the philanthropy, benevolence, and moral character of my countrymen, I am sorry to add that a spirit of scepticism and infidelity predominated in the younger part of the community, especially in the circle of those who had received what is called a good education — implying a knowledge of classical, mathematical, and metaphysical learning, as far as such knowledge can be acquired at sixteen years of age, the period when most of the writers were then appointed to India.

"My mind is at this moment solemnly impressed with scenes long past in these remote regions, especially in conversation at the breakfast-table of a gentleman, frequented by young men of the first character in the Company's civil service. Infidelity was the order of the day, the systems of Voltaire and Hume the principal topic of discourse, the philosophy of Sans Souci the grand subjects of admiration. The truths of Christianity were so entirely effaced by these doctrines, that for years together many of those deluded youths never entered a place of worship, nor read the Bible, except for the purpose of misapplying texts and selecting unconnected passages, so often and so ably refuted by all that can be urged by the force of reasoning or the extent of learning. The breakfast-party I have alluded to was principally composed of my own select friends — young men of superior talents, amiable dispositions, and elegant accomplishments. As such I loved and esteemed them: in another point of view I was happily permitted to adopt the decision of the venerable patriarch, — 'Unto their assembly, mine honour, be not thou united.'"

It would seem that the example set by the Governor-General was, as might naturally be expected, not without its effect on the community.

" Lord Mornington goes regularly to church, and professes a regard for religion. You may easily conceive the astonishment of some of the seniors at these religious proceedings. However, all was silence and decent acquiescence. It became fashionable to say that religion was a very proper thing, and that no civilised state could subsist without it. Our Christian society flourishes; merit is patronised; immoral characters are marked; and young men of good inclinations have the best opportunities of improvement."

Mr. Brown, the senior chaplain, also expresses himself favourably as to the new order of things that was beginning to arise :—

" These solemn acts, and the public thanksgivings, which took place for the first time under Marquis Wellesley's government, awakened a religious sense of things in many, and led to an open and general acknowledgment of the Divine Providence, which has been highly beneficial to the interests of true religion and virtue."

It appears evident, from these extracts, that the Anglo-Indian society was — imperceptibly, perhaps, to itself—gradually awakening from that state of apathy and indifference in which, with rare exceptions, it had hitherto remained. Still it required the presence of a person invested with direct authority, in all matters connected with the interior

arrangements and the requisite discipline of the
Church, to complete the work that was auspiciously
begun.

It was on the evening of the 28th November,
1814, that THOMAS FANSHAW MIDDLETON, the
father and founder of the Anglican Church of our
magnificent Asiatic empire, quietly stepped ashore,
with as little ceremony as the humblest cadet who
had been his fellow-passenger across the pathless
ocean. There were no noisy demonstrations of welcome from the ramparts of Fort William; there was
no gathering of smiling and obsequious expectants
at the Chandpaul Ghaut; the meteor flag of England, that "for a thousand years had braved the
battle and the breeze," streamed not forth from its
lofty staff to do honour to the new prelate; and
there was a general absence of all those "pomps
and vanities" which usually await the advent of
a great man in a far country. That the person
principally interested keenly felt the apparent discourtesy of his reception will be seen from the
following short extract from a letter he addressed to
the Rev. Mr. Norris, in which, after remarking on
"the policy to prevent the bishop from having his
proper consequence," he thus proceeds:—

" As to my reception on landing, it was anything but
what it ought to have been ; it surprised every one : so
that, on the whole, there are no prejudices in my favour.
Every thing is to depend on incessant exertion."

There was, however, no intentional disrespect, or

absence of a kindly feeling towards him, in the
apparent apathy and coldness which attended his
arrival. It was policy; it was—may we so call it—
a pusillanimous fear of alarming the religious prejudices of the natives, which any public demonstration
might, by possibility, have excited. It was, in short,
the re-echo of those anxious forebodings which some
alarmists in Parliament had put forth, and which
prophesied the most disastrous consequences, as likely
to result from a similar public display of respect towards the head of the Church as would have been, by
prescriptive usage, accorded to the chief functionary
of the law, or the commander-in-chief of the army.
It must, likewise, be remembered that that illustrious
statesman the Earl of Moira, governor-general of
India, was, at the period of the bishop's arrival,
engaged in superintending the operations of the
Nepaul war, at a great distance from the capital.
We have, therefore, a valid excuse for the apparent—
for it was not *real*— discourtesy of the subordinate
members of the government, when the alarms that
were so industriously bruited about are considered,
and the responsibility that would have attached to
them had any of the evils which had been so sagely
predicted actually occurred. Fortunately for his
country, and for the interests of the Church, the
new bishop was a man of singular prudence, fore-
thought, and discretion; and had there really been
any transient feeling of uneasiness amongst the natives, which might have caused agitation, it would

soon have passed away when they perceived, as the
more intelligent amongst them could not fail to do,
that the bent of the bishop's mind was directed
" rather to the reform of the European than to the
conversion of the native population."

We have now to witness the foundation of a
church on settled principles, under "this great and
good man," as Bishop Heber emphatically designated him in his primary charge :—

" The imperfect system of administration by military
chaplains" was now to be rectified and corrected.
Hitherto " the English clergy appeared in India, de-
tached from all connexion with an episcopal establishment. They were subject to no episcopal jurisdiction ;
they were far removed from the influence of any ecclesiastical superior ; they were the mere stipendiary servants of the Government. The authority to which they
were amenable was purely of a secular description, and
the discipline by which they were regulated approached
more nearly to a *military* than to a spiritual character."

The evil resulting from the state of things here
described had attracted the notice of that intelligent
traveller, Lord Valentia :—

" All British India," says he,* " does not afford one
episcopal see, whilst that advantage has been granted to
the province of Canada ; and yet it is certain that, from
the remoteness of the country, *and the peculiar tempta-
tions to which the freedom of manners exposes the clergy*,
immediate episcopal superintendence can nowhere be
more requisite."

* Vol. i. p. 243.

It was to reform such a state of things that the bishop assiduously applied himself; he lost as little time as possible in holding his primary visitation; and it may give some idea of the paucity of chaplains in those days, that only ten could attend without being called to Calcutta from distances of from 800 to 1000 miles, to the great inconvenience and disturbance of the public service. The charge he delivered to his clergy on this occasion is so sensible, so practical, and so happily expressed, that it will be found well worth perusal. The striking contrast presented between the actual position of the chaplains and that of the clergy at home appears to have been deeply impressed on his mind; but the prevailing sentiment with him would seem to have been that of approximating, as nearly as local circumstances would permit, to the standard that had long prevailed in our native land :—

" The model," he says, " I would propose to you is that of the English parish priest, the guardian of morals, the instructor of youth, the comforter of the afflicted, the promoter and director of works of charity and love, and the guide of all who are entrusted to his charge in the way of peace. And I anticipate all objections arising from a different condition of society, in the reply that this is still the standard to which you should endeavour to make all difficulties gradually yield. Admitting the difficulties of the case, I am still of opinion that you will not want encouragement in the endeavour.

to establish a pastoral influence, especially if it be attempted by your taking the lead in plans of benevolence and usefulness, which cannot anywhere originate so properly as with yourselves."

The sound view which Bishop Middleton took of the peculiar position and duties of the chaplains, and his earnest desire, in spite of local circumstances, and in the face of some opposition, to extend the sphere of their usefulness, and to concentrate the field of their labours, was, doubtless, attended with the most favourable result to the progress of Christianity, and the discouragement of immorality and indifference amongst the European population of his great diocese. He was fully aware of the prevalence amongst some sincere, but over-zealous persons, of a most erroneous view of his high office, and that it was considered by no means an unimportant part of his prescribed duty to be a sort of head missionary, and to be instant, " in season and out of season," in fanning and keeping alive the flame, and in pushing forward active measures for the conversion of the heathen population by whom he was surrounded. Even amongst the Court of Directors there were to be found men, whose experience should have taught them better, but who, being deeply impressed with the sublime influences of Christianity, and of its alone efficacy as a means of " saving health " to a world that lay in darkness and the shadow of death, thought the bishop on this point coming short of those enthusiastic notions in which they incontinently indulged; and were, in consequence, disposed to regard with less favour his really useful and exemplary labours. To a man so keenly sensitive to the good opinion of those he valued, so anxious to fulfil to the uttermost his allotted task, and withal so conscientious in the discharge of his episcopal functions, a knowledge of this fact could not be otherwise than painful; and, in addition to the numerous disquietudes that beset him in many quarters, must have added its weight in breaking down a naturally fine constitution. But be this as it may, these too sanguine enthusiasts had to deal with a person who, though cautious and temperate in adopting a resolution, was, as his biographer informs us, when he had once formed it, *steadfast and immoveable*. We read, accordingly,—

" That the primary object for which he came out was to govern an established Christian Church; and he conceived that his situation and his authority would have undergone no *essential* change, even if the design of spreading the Gospel among the Hindoos had been abandoned by all parties, without exception. So long as there should remain in India a community of persons already professing the Christian religion, so long would the presence of a bishop be required for its spiritual superintendence and government. To merge the pastoral in the missionary character would, therefore, be no less than virtually to desert the station which he was expressly appointed to maintain, and to change it for other grounds, which would afford him no appropriate or distinct position. On this principle it was that he was uniformly anxious to keep the duties of the clergy and those of the missionaries separate from each other, a tendency which he found it extremely difficult to counteract. In spite of all impediments, however, he felt it his duty to persevere in his resistance to it."

Since it is now an accredited fact that, when about to start on his primary visitation, dark and sinister rumours were spread by Mahomedan fakirs and others, more particularly in the south of India, that the principal object of the bishop was to carry out a scheme for the suppression of the Hindoo faith, and for the compulsory conversion of the natives to the Gospel : the wisdom and the sound policy of the course which he pursued, and to which, irrespective of the frowns of some and the ill-disguised disappointment of others, he steadily and inflexibly adhered during the whole of his valuable Indian life, cannot be too much admired. Whilst acting, if we may use such an expression, with so statesman-like a spirit, in steadily pursuing the line of conduct which he believed most conducive to the true interests of Christianity in the East, he has left in the "Bishop's Mission College," in Bengal, one of the noblest monuments to his piety and zeal, and one of the strongest proofs that, by appropriate means, and by proper instruments, he was not less keenly alive to the duty of inculcating the Gospel of

Peace, and the glorious hope of a blessed immortality, than the noisiest and most obstreperous of those who expected more than it was possible to accomplish.

We have already said that we consider it fortunate that the first Bishop of India should have been a man whose profound attachment to the Church was tempered by so much moderation and so excellent a judgment. And profound as is our respect for the memory of the highly-gifted and accomplished Bishop Heber, we question whether, with all his fine, romantic genius, his brilliant talents, his susceptible and impassioned spirit, and the superlative excellence of his unspotted life, he would have played his part so well as the founder, as he subsequently did as the conservator, of the stately building that his predecessor had reared. Even the charming simplicity of his character, and the amiability that marked his everyday actions, might, in some respects have been less advantageous than the stern and unbending bearing of the lofty churchman whom he succeeded, and who on every occasion in which what he conceived his rights and the privileges of his order were in question, acknowledged no compromise, and would hear of no concession. The views entertained by Bishop Heber are clearly expressed in one of his letters to the Hon. C. W. Wynn, and confirm that respect and admiration which all must entertain for his self-denial and unworldliness:—

" It has, indeed, been for several years a favourite day-dream of mine *to fancy myself conducting the affairs of an extended mission*, and by conciliation and caution smoothing the difficulties, and appeasing the religious quarrels and jealousies, which have hitherto chiefly opposed the progress of Christianity in the East."

And in a subsequent letter he adds, what he afterwards carried into practice,—

" I will, so far as health allows, visit every church in the diocese, though I should be compelled to go about in a single palanquin, and to stint my establishment at Calcutta to pay my travelling charges."

The humility of this passage contrasts rather forcibly with the more imposing progress of Bishop Middleton, who, we are told, with his family and suite,—

" Reclined in their respective palanquins, surrounded by guards of the native police, armed some of them with lance and target, and arrayed in picturesque and fanciful costumes, attended by tents and beds, provisions and baggage, disposed upon the backs of camels, and with an escort of regular troops as a guard of honour, under the command of an English officer."*

In some minuter points there was a difference between the two prelates, " wide as the poles asunder." Under the most sultry Bengal sun, Bishop Middleton

* An admirable selection was made of the officer in command of the escort, the present Colonel John Low, who has since risen to the highest political offices.

would never have appeared in public divested of the
smallest portion of the episcopal costume. He would
probably have indulged in a supercilious smile could
he have beheld his successor cantering cheerily along
in a wide-brimmed straw hat and white trowsers;
and however rejoiced he might have felt at the conversion of a heathen, he would have been horrified
at the idea of pursuing a snipe or a florikin.

It is, perhaps, fortunate likewise for the distinguished prelate who now fills the episcopal chair in
Bengal, that he, too, was preceded by other eminent
and enlightened men in the sultry scenes of his
arduous labours. It was our fortune to hear him
preach, about eighteen years ago, a few days before
his departure for India, and we well recollect his
bursting forth into a florid apostrophe : — " Shall I,
then, despise the Indian ?   No, he is my brother!"
We strongly surmise that the practical experience
the amiable bishop has since gained of his sable
" brother " has tended, in some degree, to convince
him that "his brother" is not exactly composed of
such malleable materials as a fervid imagination, and
the perusal, probably, of the memoirs of poor Martyn, had pictured to his overheated fancy.   No
doubt, as a man possessed of a strong mind and a
high order of intellect, he, like Bishop Middleton,
finds more profitable occupation for his time in
watching over the European community than in
prosecuting a hopeless crusade against the puerile
and debasing ceremonies, or the darker and bloody

F

stained superstitions of Hindooism. The Anglo-
Indian Church may well be proud, that in a period
of little more than thirty years she can boast of
three such hallowed names as MIDDLETON, HEBER,
WILSON; names illustrious in the annals of the East,
not less by their lives than by their devotedness to
the sacred institutions of the Protestant Episcopal
Church in Asia.

In a very old work, published in 1655, entitled
" A Voyage to East India," by Edward Terry, chaplain to Sir Thomas Roe, there are many interesting
particulars of the customs and character of the natives, and we make a short extract containing a
curious account of the Brahmins, who have been,
and still are, the most determined opponents to the
spread of Christianity:—

" Some Bramins have told me that they acknowledge one God, whom they describe with a thousand
eyes, with a thousand hands, and as many feet; that
thereby they may express his power, as being all eye
to see, and all foot to follow, and all hand to smite
offenders. The consideration whereof makes that people
very exact in the performances of all moral duties, following alone the light of Nature in their dealings with
men, most carefully observing that royal law, *in doing
nothing to others but what they would be well contented to
suffer from others.* These Bramins talk of two books,
which not long after the creation, when the world began
to be peopled (they say), were delivered by God to Bramen, one of which, containing very high, and secret,
and mysterious things, was sealed up, and might not be

opened; the other was to be read, but only by the Bramins or priests. This book, which they call the 'Shas-
ter,' or the book of their written word, was by Bramen
communicated unto Ram and Parmissan, two other
famed prophets, and hath been transcribed in all ages
ever since by the Bramins, out of which they deliver
precepts unto the people. The day of rest which they
observe as a sabbath is Thursday, as the Mahomedans do
Friday. As antiently amongst the Jews, their priesthood is hereditary, for all those Bramins' sons are
priests, and they all take the daughters of Bramins to
be their wives."

Whilst the Hindoos, therefore, had a regular
priesthood, our countrymen were for a long period
left, as it were, to take care of themselves.

" Without exaggeration it may be affirmed, that in
India, for a long period of time, the more general impression respecting our countrymen was, that they were
altogether destitute of religious sentiment or belief.
Many of the civil servants might be said to be almost in
a state of excommunication from Christian ordinances,
for twenty years together, with exception of an occasional visit to the seats of Government. Thus numbers
of young men, who received their appointments to India
at a very early age, were left wholly without public religious instruction, and consequently were in danger of
sinking, gradually and silently, into a state of virtual
apostasy."

We have one melancholy instance of this recorded
in Martyn's " Memoirs :"

" At Patna, in addition to his present perplexities, he

had the severe pain of beholding a servant of the Company, a man advanced in years, and occupying a situation of great respectability, living in a state of daring apostasy from the Christian faith, and openly professing his preference for Mahometanism. He had even built a mosque of his own, which at this season, being the Mohurrum, was adorned with flags, and being illuminated at night, proclaimed the shame of the offender."

There are numerous testimonies in all the early writers on India, to the utter deficiency of any religious observances and to the extreme paucity of chaplains, whilst, limited as the number were, we are told that, as if to aggravate the evil, " unworthy individuals were sometimes found to insinuate themselves into this sacred department of the public service." We will not dwell further on this melancholy theme than by subjoining a short extract from " The Indian Recreations," by the Rev. Dr. Tennant, who was one of His Majesty's chaplains in India, and therefore a more competent witness than any layman could be as to the state of society, in this respect, in 1798 : —

" Young persons from Europe, of little information and still less reflection, observing the puerile ceremonies of the Hindoo worship, the impositions of priestcraft, and the devout submission of ignorance, in the full extent of their enormity, begin to suppose they discover much imposture in all religious establishments, and to imagine that all stand alike on one basis, upon which the crafty have raised a superstructure to overawe the

timid and to ensnare the weak. Full of such notions,
which they find countenanced in society under the
appellation of liberality of sentiment, they fancy that to
be lax in principle is to become liberal in mind; and
that to ridicule religion is a sufficient title to make them
be ranked with the wise. But when the restraints of
religion are once overthrown, the ties of virtue and duty
are also soon broken. In remote districts, where persons of this description have sometimes been invested
with command, there is no doubt that the looseness of
their conduct has too nearly corresponded with these
principles. That the Court of Directors were not aware
of the necessity of supporting the interests of religion
and virtue among their servants, in a country where
distance deprives them, in a great measure, of efficient
control over them, it would be rashness to affirm. It
is, however, certain, that neither the number nor choice
of the clergymen they have appointed in Bengal has
been in proportion to the number of their servants
nor the importance of the object in view; whether you
regard keeping up the appearance of religion among
Europeans, or disseminating its principles among the
natives. In Bengal the full complement of chaplains is
only nine; their actual number seldom exceeds five or
six. Two of these being always fixed at the Presidency,
, all the other European stations, dispersed over a tract of
country much more extensive than Great Britain, are
committed to the charge of the other three or four individuals. There are a few others at Madras and Bombay; but altogether there is too small a number to keep
up the restraints of decency and religion in a society
constituted like that of the Europeans in India. As a
necessary result the presence of a clergyman is seldom

seen, or even expected, to solemnize the usual ceremonies of marriages, baptisms, or funerals.   Prayers are
read *sometimes* at the stations where a chaplain hap-
pened to reside; but *I have seldom heard of any sermon
delivered*, except by His Majesty's chaplains and those
at Calcutta.   Hence it must often happen that many
persons have left England at an early age, and resided·
in India perhaps for twenty or thirty years, without
once having heard divine service till their return.   It
is, surely, not to be wondered at, that religious and
moral duties should be forgotten in a country where
their utility is never inculcated, nor the necessity, even
of their appearance, enforced.   With irreligious principles irregular conduct is intimately connected. Gaming,
debauchery, and all kinds of extravagance in living, are
generally in its train. The man whose fortune has been
ruined by dissipation, or at a gaming-table, is certainly
not the most likely to withstand temptation in the execution of his duty.   On the contrary, those whose profligate habits have reduced them to distress have in
general been the only persons who have attempted to
retrieve their affairs at the expense either of the Company or of the native inhabitants.   In the end, therefore, the economy of the Court of Directors in consti-
tuting their religious establishments may appear to be
founded on false principles.   The whole charge incurred
for religious duties, both to the European inhabitants
and natives of Bengal, does not amount to a sum nearly
equal to the monthly salary paid to some individuals in
their service.   The small emolument held out to the
clerical profession affords, perhaps, another instance in
which prudential considerations defeat their own purpose.   Men of decent conduct and respectability of cha-

racter cannot be supposed w.lling, for a trivial salary; to embark for a part of the world so distant as India, where they must bid adieu to all hopes of preferment at home; while the service in which they embark offers only present subsistence, but holds out no gradation of rank or emolument. For an appointment in India such men rarely apply; and as often as characters of a contrary description are sent there, they invariably do more harm than good. Clergymen who engage in all the fashionable dissipations of the country are ill calculated to support the dignity of religion among their countrymen, and little likely to withdraw the natives from their errors. The standard of truth will, if committed to such hands, be but feebly upheld, or perhaps altogether disgraced; and in either case it will always be accompanied by few followers. Since writing the above, the evils complained of have, to a certain extent, been corrected; yet many, it is to be feared, from the prevalence of long habit, from indolence, or from contempt of the sacred institutions of their country, have wilfully neglected the opportunity, when offered, of attending on the offices of religion."—*Indian Recreations,* vol. i. p. 94.

The settlers in India were not, however, even at a very early period of our connexion with it, entirely destitute of clerical ministration. The Rev. J. S. M. Anderson, in his valuable "History of the Colonial Church," has traced to a very remote period the progress of the Protestant religion in the East. He contrasts unfavourably the languid and disjointed efforts made in those early times by this country with the connected plans, the excellent arrange-

ments, the uncompromising fervour, and the prose-
lyting zeal of the Portuguese, who forced upon the
natives of the Peninsula and Ceylon; and wherever
their settlements extended, the doctrines of the
Romish faith, and who, amongst the ruins of the
once princely Goa, have left some splendid memorials
of the grandeur and the magnificence of the Catholic
Church. We learn from him, that

"In 1653–4, the agent and council of Fort St. George
were raised to the rank of a presidency. The Portuguese Church at St. Thomé — whatever may have been
the indiscreet zeal of those who ministered before her
altar — was a witness, at least, that they who worshipped
there were not ashamed to hold up the symbols of their
faith before the eyes of the natives of India. How long
the Christians of Fort St. George, who boasted that they
were free from the superstitions of the Popish Portuguese, could bear to see the extension of their com-
merce, and the increase of their secular power, and yet
remain without exhibiting any public evidence that they
too were the servants of the same Lord, will be seen
hereafter."

Mr. Anderson appends a list of "Chaplains in India,"
embracing a period from 1667 to 1700. The total
number is twenty-three; but it appears that one of
them declined his office, and another was, on account
of some irregularities, removed. Of the remainder,
four were nominated to Bombay, four for Surat,
three for India generally, three for Fort St. George,
two for Bengal, three for St. Helena, and two for

Bantam. They must, therefore, have been attached
to the factories severally established at these places,
with exception of those for India, who probably accompanied governors or chiefs of the Council. In
the " Memoir of the Rev. C. Buchanan " in 1805, at
which period nearly twenty thousand of His Majesty's
troops were employed in India, besides several thousand European troops in the Company's service, he
states the number of chaplains to have been six for
Bengal, five for Madras, and four for Bombay; and
that in the whole of the British possessions under
the sway of the Company there were *but three
churches.* The year previously to Bishop Middleton's
appointment (1813) there had been a considerable increase in the chaplains, although still very
inadequate in number, to supply the wants even of
the European soldiery. We find from the published
list that there were in Bengal fifteen chaplains, but
amongst them appears the name of Henry Martyn,
who died in Persia in 1812 ; at Madras thirteen, and
in Bombay five; certainly a more respectable muster-
roll, and one more approximating to the exigencies
of the European population, for the most considerable
part of whom (His Majesty's troops) the Company
had entered into a stipulation to provide. But if the
chaplains were increased, there appears to have been
very little solicitude evinced, as to the means of per-
forming public worship, with the solemnity which
ought to attach to it. A mess-room, an empty bar-

rack, the official court-house of the magistrate, or, in short, any building that could be temporarily applied to the purpose, was considered sufficient. A minute of the Bengal government in 1807, affords a curious illustration of the state of things we have attempted to convey to our readers :—

" The commander-in-chief has directed a riding-school to be included in the estimates for public buildings at Meerut, upon the scale of the riding-schools at Ghazeepoor and Cawnpore, *for the double purpose of a place of worship and a riding-school.*"

In the correspondence of Bishop Middleton and Bishop Heber with official men, both in India and in England, the almost entire want of churches at the large military stations up the country, forms a subject of incessant and reiterated complaint. We will quote, however, only one glaring instance, in an extract of a letter from Bishop Heber to Mr. Charles Lushington, the present member for Westminster, and who was then secretary to the Supreme Government in Bengal :—

" *Benares, September* 6, 1824.

" Ghazeepoor is in grievous want of a church, or rather will be, as soon as it has a chaplain. The present building is in a hopeless state of decay — so much so, that when I mentioned my intention of preaching in it, I was assured that nobody would venture their lives ' *sub iisdem trabibus;*' and *I was obliged to borrow an auction-room in the neighbourhood.*"

It is gratifying to know that this grievance has been effectually remedied; and at the time we are writing, we believe there is not a station in any part of India, which is the head-quarters of a European regiment, where there is not a church and a resident chaplain.

The almost total impossibility of suitably providing for the celebration of Divine worship at the great military stations, from the very inadequate number of chaplains, had been continually pressed on the home authorities; and as did Bishop Middleton, so we find Bishop Heber losing no opportunity of earnestly requesting attention to this point.

" We are sadly off for clergy in India," writes Bishop Heber to Mr. John Thornton in 1824, " though I fear the Directors themselves cannot altogether remedy the apparent aversion which young men in England entertain to this service and this climate. Yet this aversion seems to me extremely unfounded; and I am sure that a man of gentlemanly manners and real zeal for religion, will find few situations where he will meet with more kindness and attention, and be more useful, than as chaplain to a civil or military station in Bengal."

Again we find him, in a letter to Dr. Phillimore, thus expressing himself:—

" The clergymen whom I have seen or corresponded with are very respectable, and many of them intelligent and well informed. I only wish *there were more of them* in the country, but their paucity is really most grievous. Many very important stations are at this moment as effectually cut off as if they were in the centre of China. Even in Calcutta and the neighbouring stations, though some of the clergy officiate three times a-day, and though I myself and the archdeacon work as hard and as regularly as any of ' the *labouring* clergy ' (to use the modish phrase) in any part of the world, we could not get the Sunday duty done without resorting to the aid of the missionaries. With these last I have good reason to be satisfied. They all cheerfully (such, of course, as are of the Church of England) have received licenses, and submitted themselves to my authority."

About the same period that Dr. Tennant wrote, there is a curious dispatch from the Court of Directors to the Government of Madras, dated 25th May, 1798, quoted by Hough,* which, though written in general in an excellent spirit, and inculcating sound and correct principles, is yet amusing from the tradesmanlike desire it evinces to turn to a profitable account in the ledger " the increasing spirit of luxury and dissipation in our principal settlements, and even at some of the subordinate stations."

In the concluding paragraph of this despatch a very significant hint is thrown out that this state of things may originate in too much affluence, and too large salaries; in other words, the laxity of morals and indifference to religious matters of the Anglo-Indian society of that day, is put prominently forward as a valid reason for the commencement of that system of paring and clipping which, more particu-

* "History of Christianity in India," vol. iv. p. 186.

larly as regards the military allowances, was shortly afterwards commenced, and which provoked strong and indignant remonstrances from the then Governor-general, the princely-minded Marquis of Wellesley.

In quoting the following severe strictures by the Honourable Mr. Shore, in his excellent work, "Notes on Indian Affairs," we would preface them with an explanatory remark. It is evident that Mr. Shore wrote under a full impression that our country-men of those days voluntarily surrendered themselves to the attractive doctrine of the Epicurean philoso-phers, quoted by St. Paul in his Epistle to the Corinthians, "Let us eat and drink, for to-morrow we die."

Although a nice and accurate observer in general, we are fain to think that in this instance Mr. Shore formed his judgment too hastily, and without taking into consideration various connecting causes, which, viewed conjointly, tended to produce the lamentable state of things which he has painted in so sombre a tint.

" The habits of the English in this country, till within the last twenty years, were, as far as religion is con-cerned, far below the heathen by whom they were sur-rounded. These, at least, paid attention to their own forms and ceremonies ; but the English appear to have considered themselves at liberty to throw aside all con-siderations on the subject. Their conduct has been repeatedly alluded to by the natives, in reply to those missionaries and clorgymen who have attempted to make converts among them. The son of the Nuwab of the Carnatic said to Swartz one day, ' Padre, we always regarded you Europeans as a most irreligious race of men, unacquainted even with the nature of prayer, till you came and told us you had good people among you in Europe. Since you came here, indeed, we begin to think better of you.' When, at a later period, Dubois explained to the people the virtues inculcated by the Christian religion. they constantly asked him why he did not teach the Europeans, who had none of those virtues ; and the same question is often put to the clergy and missionaries of the present day.

" A great improvement has certainly taken place of late years ; but though the tone of speaking and think- ing on religious subjects has been raised, the practical effect of the principles which are professed is by no means so general as is commonly believed ; and though the affectation of infidelity has descended (with many other vices and follies which were formerly considered fashionable) to the lowest ranks of society, and to scoff or sneer at religion is looked upon equally as a proof of ignorance and bad taste, I doubt whether the present generation of the Indu-English have advanced much in the essentials of Christianity beyond their fathers. If they have ceased openly to outrage religion, they give very few proofs that they have any sincere regard to its dictates. Very few attend the service of the Church, and still fewer are in the habits of private prayer or reading the Bible. Too many, indeed, come under Johnson's definition of infidels, or, in his own em- phatic language, ' They are infidels, as dogs are—they never think about it.' I have heard of a military officer of high rank, who, so far from ever entering a church, or attending Divine service, usually spent the Sunday in cock-fighting. What must the private soldiers, who were perfectly well acquainted with the mode in which his Sundays were passed, think on receiving an order to march to church? They, indeed, are not backward at imitating the example of their superiors, having generally little sense of religion themselves.

"There is certainly little in the conduct of the English, whether the Government or individuals be concerned, which should induce the people of India to respect the religion professed by us. Money has been the object; and to realise this, justice and the interests of the people have been sacrificed; and to such a height has the worship of Mammon been carried, that the common language of the natives in speaking of us is, 'As for the English, if you have a hungry dog you must feed him: there is nothing to be got out of an Englishman without paying him well in some way or other.' Is it likely, with such sentiments towards us, and observing the almost entire neglect which we exhibit to the ordinances of our religion, that they should form a favourable opinion of that which we profess to entertain? The mass of the people, indeed, consider the English as a low tribe *who have no religion;* and that to become of the same persuasion as ourselves, they have only to throw off the trammels of *caste,* to drink wine, not forgetting occasionally to get drunk, and eat beef or pork. It is not many years ago since the Government of Bombay declined, for a considerable period, to erect a church at one of their stations, for fear of annoying the prejudices of the people; thus, not only to their disgrace, be it said, showing how little they cared about religion, *but evincing a want of knowledge of the native character on this point :* for the religious feelings of both Hindoos and Moossulmans are such, that the more those of any other creed attend to their own religious doctrines and ceremonies, the more will they be really respected by the mass of the people of India."

Having given this rather long extract from Mr. Shore, we will give a short one from the Rev. Mr. Buchanan, who says in his "Memoir on a Colonial Ecclesiastical Establishment :" *——

" Were we, on the other hand, to state particularly the regard paid by our countrymen to Christian ministration, *wherever regularly afforded*, it would be an additional argument for granting the means of affording it. Wherever the Christian minister solicits attention, he finds an audience. In whatever part of British India he is stationed, *there will be a disposition to respect the religion of early life*, when its public ordinances shall have been revived."

There is a striking fact in the life of Bishop Middleton illustrative of this point :—

" Before the bishop left Cochin, the sacrament was administered to forty persons by Archdeacon Loring ; and it appears that this holy rite had not been celebrated at that place for twenty years before."

Although no allowance was made for travelling on visitation, Archdeacon Barnes at Bombay, and Archdeacon Robinson at Madras, adopted the plan,

* "Memoir," p. 3.

previous to the appointment of bishops, of voluntarily, and at their own expense, visiting every station at which a chaplain was resident. Considering how anomalous a position chaplains were formerly in, this practice of personal inspection of districts could not fail to be productive of the best effects. Some years since the Annual Mutiny Act entirely left out the clauses upon which the claim for including under military control the chaplains in India was founded. But another inconvenience was found to arise, which had probably been overlooked; for after these gentlemen were released from the interference of the head of the army, so ill-defined was the power vested in the bishop, that it proved inoperative in practice. In one very grave case, which occurred about fifteen years ago, after trying without success to put in operation the machinery of his Consistorial Court, the bishop was necessitated to have recourse to the extra-judicial power of the Supreme Government; and by these means alone he was enabled to cause a chaplain, whose conduct had given rise to great scandal, and to much injury to the cause of religion, to be removed from his station and sent to England. We have here an ample proof that the administration of ecclesiastical law, not perhaps practically the most simple and satisfactory even in England, with the advantage of a legal body expert from habit in dealing with its intricacies and explaining its provisions, is in a foreign country, where its study is merely incidental, loaded with peculiar difficulties.

We find Lord Broughton stating, in moving the second reading of the Marriages (India) Bill, on the 16th May, 1851 :—

" At present the ministers of all religions in India, capable of solemnising marriages, were only 1015 in number. This was but a scanty supply for so extensive a continent. Certain laymen had been consequently authorised to celebrate marriages. under the permission and license of the Governor-general. Unfortunately, the marriages celebrated by these laymen were the marriages most generally questioned. So late as the year 1849, in the Supreme Court of Bombay, an attempt was made to quash an action for *crim. con.*, on the ground that a marriage so solemnised was no marriage at all ; but in that case the Court held that the marriage was good and valid. In a similar case, however. in the Supreme Court of Bombay, such a marriage was held to be null and invalid. There were, at present, only six ministers of the Free Kirk of Scotland in India ; and every one of the marriages celebrated by those clergymen might be questioned."

What a state of matters, as affecting the peace and happiness of families, and the rights and property of individuals, is here disclosed ! It was one of those subjects, in connexion with the ministration of the Church, which painfully forced itself on the notice of Bishop Heber. In a letter, dated Madras, March 1826, and addressed to Archdeacon Hautine, as to the hardships to which soldiers and the followers of a camp, are liable in consequence of some chaplains

refusing to marry them without the usual prelimina-
ries of banns or license, he says :—

" I find that till that injunction (by Bishop Middleton)
was issued, it was the uniform practice of chap'ains in
India to celebrate such military marriages without banns,
or any other lisence than a written permission from the
officer commanding the regiment to which the parties
belonged — a practice which, I understand, is also followed by His Majesty's chaplains, when attached to
corps on foreign service ; and which, therefore, by a
parity of circumstances, may seem no less allowable in
these remote and newly-conquered countries. It appears,
too, that a compliance with the letter of the canons has
been found actually impossible in many parts of India ;
and that, more particularly in the upper provinces of the
Presidency of Bengal, the chaplains have continued their
former practice. Bishop Middleton's injunctions to the
contrary notwithstanding."

" Our deplorable want of clergy," writes Bishop Wilson in April 1842, " has long lain as a heavy burden on
the minds of all thinking and devout persons in this
country. Above half our stations are destitute of clergy
to celebrate Divine worship, to administer holy sacraments, to preach the Gospel, to visit the sick and dying,
and to perform the solemn offices of piety over the remains of the departed."

Can we feel surprise, in such a state of things, at
the difficulties which were interposed to the due and
legal solemnisation of marriages, and the disputes
to which the imperfect performance of them gave
rise ?

Bishop Middleton, after expressing his satisfaction that " a respect for the ordinances of religion is evidently gaining ground," deplores the paucity of chaplains, and says (1822) :—

" At this moment a large proportion of the Christian subjects of this Government are virtually excommunicated, for they have not the use of the sacraments or the common offices of religion. It was, indeed, an oversight, which required the Company to maintain a bishop in their territories without making it imperative upon them to keep up a body of clergy."

And in his Charge to his clergy in 1821, he says : —

" Humanly speaking, every thing is against us. We are called upon to work a change in the habits, the hearts, and the very nature of man, in circumstances of peculiar difficulty, and to build up a Zion unto God in the waste places of the earth."

A very intelligent lady, Mrs. Elwood, thus expresses herself : —

" There are but few churches, considering that the English have been established in this part of India for more than two centuries. It has been justly observed, that if we were driven out of the country to-morrow, few vestiges would remain at those places where the English have settled as evidence of their ever having been under Christian rule. The Portuguese have evinced far more zeal for the honour of their God, and for the propagation of Christianity, than the English. It is said there have been instances of officers who have been at stations for years, where there was no place of religious worship and no chaplains. Surely, under such circumstances, young men whose principles are not quite fixed must run the risk of totally forgetting whatever instructions they may have received in their early years."

We have given the sentiments of this lady, as, though they do not excuse, they in some degree palliate, the tendency to indifference and infidelity noticed by Mr. Shore. For surely the extreme disadvantage in which our young countrymen *were* (we are, fortunately, able to speak in the past tense) placed, should not be altogether lost sight of in forming an opinion of their character, if we would desire to judge fairly, and hold the balance even between their opportunities and their shortcomings. We find from the " Life of Bishop Heber," that it was not the fault but the misfortune of the out-stations that they were left so destitute of clerical assistance : —

" The applications for resident chaplains from the inhabitants of many of the principal stations which the Bishop received, occasioned him much painful uneasiness : they were but too generally such as he had it not in his power to flatter with the least hope of receiving a favourable answer from Government. A considerable number of Europeans were either entirely debarred from the ordinances of their religion, or obliged to take long and expensive journeys to the nearest station of a resident clergyman. From six stations within the Presidency of Fort William, the Bishop received during his visitation most pressing demands for resident mission-

aries, with an assurance that every assistance and encouragement would be given them ; while to only two or
three was he able to assign even the occasional services
of the nearest chaplain."

We find the Bishop soon after writing in this
strain, when on his visitation tour :—

" The eagerness and anxiety for more chaplains is
exceedingly painful to witness, knowing, as I well do,
that the remedy of the evil is beyond the power of
Government to supply. Not Westmorland before the
battle of Agincourt wished with greater earnestness for
' more men from England' than I do."

Some of the inconveniences resulting from this
deficiency are forcibly pointed out in the extract
from his " Journal," dated 5 July, 1824 : —

" I met a lady to-day who had been several years at
Nusserabad in Rajpotana, and during seven years of
her stay in India, had never seen a clergyman or had
an opportunity of going to church. This was, however, a less tedious excommunication than has been the
lot of a very good and religious man resident at Tis-
serah, who was for nineteen consecutive years the only
Christian within seventy miles, and at least 300 from
any place of worship. Occasionally he has gone to
receive the sacrament at Chittagong, about as far from
his residence as York from London. These are sad
stories, yet, I hope, not beyond the reach of a remedy."

We have already quoted a sentence of the Duke of
Wellington's ; but the whole dispatch in which it oc-
curs is so admirable in its spirit, so remarkable for

that clear and lucid arrangement which marks all his compositions, and which, in its neatness and simplicity — and, more than all, in its spirit — is so honourable to a writer who is destined to live in the memory of all generations, that we subjoin a short extract from it.* It will be readily conceded that, of all men living, the illustrious Duke is the very last to be acted upon by a pharisaical affectation of what he did not feel; and important as are his sentiments on every subject connected with the discipline of the

* " *Cartaxo, February* 6, 1811.

" I believe that you have attended a good deal to the establishment of the chaplains to the army, upon which I am now about to trouble you.

"'I have one excellent young man in this army, Mr. B—, who is attached to head-quarters, and who has never been one moment absent from his duty : excepting Mr. Denis at Lisbon, who was absent all last year, I believe Mr. B— is the only chaplain doing duty.

" I am very anxious upon this subject, not only from the desire which every man must have, that so many persons as there are in this army should have the advantage of religious instruction, *but from a knowledge that it is the greatest support and aid to military discipline and order.*

" It has, besides, come to my knowledge, that Methodism is spreading very fast in the army. There are two, if not three, Methodist meetings in this town, of which one is in the Guards. The men meet in the evening and sing psalms ; and I believe a sergeant (Stephens) now and then gives them a sermon. Mr. B— has his eye upon these transactions, and would give me notice were they growing into anything that ought to be put a stop to ; and the *respectability of his character and conduct has given him an influence over these people*, which will prevent them from going wrong.

" These meetings likewise prevail in other parts of the army.

army, they derive additional value when they are
found in entire accordance with the views of men
who, from their sacred calling, are necessarily of a
graver and more serious cast of mind. If the gallant Duke, with a glance of his eagle eye, perceived
the benefit likely to result from the presence of educated, intelligent, and responsible chaplains, with an
army engaged in a stirring campaign, where every
succeeding day brought forth its storied calendar,
where there were continually new scenes to be

In the 9th Regiment there is one, at which two officers attend ;
and the commanding officer of the regiment has not been able to
prevail upon them to discontinue this practice. Here, under
similar circumstances, *we want the assistance of a respectable
clergyman.* By his personal influence and advice, and by that
of true religion, he would moderate the zeal and enthusiasm of
these gentlemen, and would prevent their meetings from being
mischievous, if he did not prevail upon them to discontinue them
entirely.

" This is the only mode in which, in my opinion, we can touch
these meetings. The meeting of soldiers in their cantonments
to sing psalms, or hear a sermon read by one of their comrades,
is, in the abstract, perfectly innocent ; and it is a better way of
spending their time than many others to which they are ad-
dicted : but it may become otherwise ; and yet, till the abuse has
made some progress, the commanding officer would have no
knowledge of it, nor could he interfere. Even at last his interference must be guided by discretion, otherwise he will do more
harm than good ; and it can in no case be so effectual as that of
a respectable clergyman. I wish, therefore, you would turn your
attention a little more to this subject, and arrange some plan by
which the number of respectable and efficient clergymen with
this army may be increased.

" WELLINGTON."

" Lieut.-Gen, Calvert,"

viewed, fresh dangers to be encountered; where the
mind, equally with the body, was kept in all the
hurry of motion and all the fever of excitement—
how much more value must attach to the same body
in the far-off East? How much more conducive to
" discipline and order," amidst the wearisomeness of
Indian ordinary military life, where, even with the
most active spirits, there is a continual tendency to
indolence and mental sluggishness; where there is
little in the comparative monotony of a distant garrison or cantonment to call forth the dormant energies of the mind, or to arouse the half-slumbering
faculties from their listless repose; how much more
beneficial to both the temporal happiness and the
eternal welfare of the soldier must be the presence
of a respectable and respected chaplain! Of the
great benefit derived from such a source we have a
most pleasing account in Mrs. Elwood's narrative,
who has feelingly described such a one as may well
be considered a model of an Indian chaplain :—

" Mr. and Mrs. Gray arrived some time after ourselves; and in this remote and dark corner of the world
you cannot conceive how inestimably valuable we found
their society; and, surrounded by heathens, how very de-
lightful it was to be able to attend Divine service. *It
was performed in one of the mess-rooms;* for, though
the Roman Catholics, fewer in numbers, and of very
inferior station to ourselves, had erected a small chapel
for their own use, *the English had never thought of
building a church.* Whilst C— was in power he did

his utmost to support and assist our excellent and worthy chaplain in several of his projects for the improvement of the society, both Christian and heathen. Schools were set on foot, a library established, and the erection of a church suggested to the Government. Mr. Gray's exertions show how much an individual, whose heart is really concerned in an undertaking, can effect. Abandoning his former pursuits for the purpose, he has applied himself to the acquirement of Oriental languages, and he is now endeavouring to reduce the Cutekee jargon into a regular form, and is translating the Scriptures into that tongue. To learning and general information he unites a warm and unaffected piety, a primitive simplicity of manners, and a benevolence of disposition, which endear him to all those who are well acquainted with him; and I have been informed that the late Bishop James expressed his warm admiration of the rare union of zeal and discretion which appeared in his character and conduct. Were there many clergymen resembling him in India, a general reformation of morals and manners might be expected."

In this, we think we may venture to term it, elegant picture of an Indian chaplain, we can be at no loss to trace the influence and powerful effect which the presence and ministrations of men of a similar stamp must exercise on the mass of a society, "where," as Bishop Heber says, "the early age at which the officers leave England, the little control to which they are afterwards subjected, and the very few opportunities afforded to most of them of ever hearing a sermon or joining in public prayer, might be expected *to heathenise them even far more than we find is the case.*"

We have another affecting instance of the benefits resulting from the labours of a pious clergyman in Forbes's " Oriental Memoirs," vol. iii. p. 54 :—

" When I was a youth, a ship from England bound to Bengal unexpectedly arrived at Bombay, with a number of passengers for Calcutta ; among them was a venerable clergyman, eminent for his talents and piety : he preached only once, after having been a fortnight on the island, and taken pains to study the character of the European inhabitants. He selected his text from the solemn address to the church at Ephesus on forgetting her first love : and applied it to the false philosophy which then pervaded the different classes of society. The discourse was such as became a faithful teacher, replete with sound reasoning, great earnestness, and affectionate solicitude. The application, especially to the younger part of the audience, was conciliatory, pathetic, and impressive. This excellent minister preached no more : he was the next day seized with an illness which soon terminated his earthly career. Such a pastor was suddenly taken away, while shepherds of a different description were left to feed the flock in the wilderness ; for India might then be termed a spiritual wilderness, compared with the steady progress of religious societies in Europe. What inestimable good may be done in India by prudent and zealous labourers in this neglected vineyard, Swartz, Gerecke, and others have clearly evinced."

It may not be inappropriate, in this place, to

chronicle a passing record of the exemplary conduct
of a regiment which, though not mowed down in the
glorious battle-field, amidst " all the pride and circumstance of war," as was the 74th at Assaye,
and more recently the 24th at Chillingwallah, yet
perished in the service of their country by trea-
chery and savage blood-thirstiness, when entangled
amidst the wintry snows and mountain fastnesses of
Affghanistan.

" While the 44th was at Dinapoer," says Bishop
Heber, " an admirable example was set by Colonel Mor-
rison and his officers ; and the men themselves were
most of them patterns of decent conduct and regular
attendance in church, not only in the morning, but in
the evening, *at which time their attendance was perfectly
voluntary.*"

Although it cannot be denied that the Government
and the East India Company were acted upon in the
first instance, to a certain extent, by the pressure
from without, it would yet be an act of injustice to
the Company were we not to admit that, severely
pressed upon as their treasury has been of late
years by the enormous expenses of the recent wars
in the north of India and in China, they have, nevertheless, provided a Church Establishment amply
sufficient for the wants of the European community
in India. Irrespective of merely religious considerations, it would be superfluous to say, that the dis-
persion of nearly a hundred and thirty clergymen
amongst the scattered stations of the Indian army,

all of them gentlemen, many of them elegant and
accomplished scholars, and the whole, with scarcely
an exception, exhibiting in their own lives a bright
example of the precepts they are commissioned to
inculcate, has been attended with the happiest results. Of course, in those classes of society in which
from their station and position they more immedi-
ately moved, they cannot fail to exercise a considerable influence. But there is every reason to believe
that the newly-awakened feeling, kindled into life by
their example and exhortation, has extended far beyond the mere polished pillars of the social edifice;
that their ministrations in the hospital, and in attendance on the sick bed of the humble soldier, have
often been blessed with the happiest results; and
that many of this class, with renovated health, owe
their recovery from brutal and degrading vices, and
the honest pride which they have subsequently felt
in pursuing a course more befitting an immortal
being, to the sensible advice, the earnest endeavours,
and the pious labours of the worthy *padre*. The
reader must not, however, suppose that the chaplain's duties are confined merely to the Sunday service, to the hospital, or even to the schools. Considering how very largely the Anglo-Indian population
have of late years increased, and that there now
spread throughout India hundreds of European
families, over whom the lights and shades of this
ever-revolving life are continually passing, sometimes
the bright sunbeam darting its glorious rays on a

happy home, and anon a dark cloud bursting, as it were, with the startling crash of the thunder-cloud over a devoted family, the inappreciable advantages of the numerous resident clergy need scarcely be enumerated. We know that there is an instinctive delicacy about the female mind which causes it to lean much on usage and prescription, and to shrink from any innovation on long-cherished opinions, which are hallowed and confirmed by religious feel- ings; and although marriage is now made by the law a civil contract merely, very few are found, even in Europe, to take advantage of it. Hence to a large proportion of society, and to ladies more parti- cularly, the propinquity of a clergyman is not only desirable, but is a source of satisfaction, of hope, of consolation. The timid bride, far apart it may be from the loved companions of her girlish days, and from those smiling and affectionate family faces that greeted her graceful advance to womanhood, as she approaches that altar in a land of strangers where she is to plight her irrevocable troth, treads with a firmer step, and feels a more sustained conviction of being enabled faithfully to fulfil the solemn vow she is to pronounce, when it is administered to her by the minister of the church of her early days. The happy mother, in the pride of her youth and beauty, as she presents her first-born to be received into the bosom of the Church, enjoys an inward satisfaction in the thought that her child has been welcomed into the flock, and the sign of the cross implanted on

its little smiling forehead, by one who has been consecrated to the service of his God. And when the
last solemn scene has arrived,—when the dark fune-
real train winds slowly along, with the measured
tread, and the muffled drum, and the mournful
strains that accompany the departed to his last
home, the chaplain awaits at the entrance of the *now*
consecrated cemetery the beloved remains that are
to be returned to their parent earth. And when all
is over, and the bereaved mourners regain the house
of desolation, they feel consoled with "sure and certain hope" that the body that now sleepeth shall
one day "awake and arise from the dead;" and that
those inspired words of the most beautiful and
affecting service that ever was composed, have been
pronounced over the narrow grave by a minister of
the invisible but omnipresent Creator of the world,
by a servant of the God of the living and of the
dead.

In the diary of the Rev. Mr. Allen, who accompanied the Bombay division into Affghanistan in
1842, we have a very graphic representation of a
soldier's funeral when on active service : —

"But the sorrows of this dismal day were not yet
over : there remained the melancholy office of commit-
ting our poor friends to the grave ; we were to march in
the morning, and it could not be delayed. It was desirable, also, that the spot should be carefully concealed,
as the Affghans frequently dig up, and cast from their
graves, the bodies of Feringhees. It was dug in the

inside of a tent, and at half-past ten, P.M., they were laid side by side ; the earth was made perfectly smooth, and a quantity of bhoosa burnt over the place, to give it the appearance of a watch-fire having been there. As many of their friends as could be got together were assembled, and as we proceeded silently down the cavalry lines, — for we were too much oppressed by sorrow at such a blank in the corps to speak even in whispers, — the accordance of almost every feature in the scene with Wolfe's beautiful elegy on Sir John Moore, struck me forcibly. No sound was heard but the slow footfall of the party ; ' We spake not a word of sorrow.' A single lantern pointed out the path, and the moon was just rising dim and sickly through the mists on the horizon. ' No useless coffins confined their breasts,' for the mangled remains were wrapt in their bedding ; and as the solemn service proceeded, we could hear in the distance an occasional shot from the pickets. What a day ! Could my friends at home realise it, surely they would prize more highly their peaceful Sabbath blessings."

We have a counterpart to this affecting narrative in Sir John Burgoyne's account of the funeral of General Fraser, who fell gloriously in the American war in 1777 :—

" About sunset the corpse of General Fraser was brought up the hill, attended only by the officers who had lived in his family. To arrive at the redoubt it passed within view of the greatest part of both armies. General Phillips, General Raidesdel, and myself, who were standing together, were struck with the humility of the procession. They who were ignorant that privacy had been requested, might construe it into neglect; we could neither endure that reflection, nor indeed restrain our natural propensity to pay our last attention to his remains. The incessant cannonade during the solemnity; the steady attitude and unaltered voice with which the chaplain officiated, though frequently covered with dust, which the shot threw up on all sides of him: the mute but expressive mixture of sensibility and indignation upon every countenance: these objects to the last of life will remain upon the mind of every man who was present. The growing duskness added to the scenery, and the whole marked a character of that juncture that would make one of the finest subjects for the pencil of a master that the field ever exhibite l."

To some few, perhaps, of colder temperament, these duties, which appertain to the chaplain, and which in a large military cantonment are continually occurring, may appear to be but of secondary importance, but to by far the greater number they will be considered of more value than our poor description can adequately convey.

The Duke of Wellington, as we have seen, deprecated the evil effects likely to attend the spread of *Methodism* in the army, judging, no doubt, that the inflated state of mind and rhapsodical flights which carry its professors far beyond the sober realities of this "work-a-day" world, would, in the end, clash with the claims of discipline and order; and that a soldiery, taught to look up to an ideal standard of religious practice, and told that it alone was genuine, would gradually come to consider their officers as

H

walking in a wrong path, and would, consequently, be disposed to treat them with less deference and to regard them with less respect.

As instances in point, we may extract a passage or two from Backhouse's " Visit to the Mauritius :"—

" We breakfasted with two young officers of the Royal Engineers, who, though awakened to the sense of the importance of a religious life, had not had the eyes of their understanding sufficiently enlightened to *see the inconsistency of a military profession* with the character of a *disciple of the Prince of Peace.*"

In another passage we likewise find the same sentiment expressed :—

" We breakfasted with two pious young officers of the Rifle Corps. These young men had been brought to a sense of the love of Christ, *but they had not apprehended the inconsistency of the military profession with Christianity.*"

Surely, on reading these passages, whilst giving every credit to the worthy missionary for the sincerity of his convictions, we cannot but admire the sagacity of the Duke of Wellington in endeavouring to check the spread of *Methodism* in the army of the Peninsula. We are subsequently informed, that " it is supposed not one person in a hundred attends a place of worship in the Mauritius ;" but if the doctrine we have seen applied to the officers was to be promulgated generally to the troops, we cannot see that they could derive much benefit from listening to admonitions which would set the more serious and better disposed to thinking on the lawfulness of that profession to which they had devoted themselves.

Without mentioning the well-known biography of Colonel Gardiner, which might be supported by many other instances, ancient and modern, we would remind this gentleman of our Saviour's answer to the soldiers in the 3d chapter of St. Luke, ver. 14, and the affecting narrative of the Centurion in the 7th chapter of the same Evangelist, in neither of which can we discover any proscription of the military profession.

Mr. Gericke, a man noted for his sincerity and for the faithful discharge of his missionary labours, did not consider it at variance with the sacred occupation to which he had devoted himself to procure a cadetship for his son, who served with credit for many years in the Madras army, and died a field officer.

In "Letters by a Lady" from Madras, which, the "Quarterly Review" says, "tells us more of what everybody cares to know than any other work that has ever appeared from India," we find another instance of the evil effects of zeal, when untempered by discretion :—

"We have had a good deal of trouble with the school lately, which is very vexatious, because it really was going on beautifully. But a little while ago, there came to Rajahmundry a Mr. G——, a dissenting missionary, a conceited, show-off sort of person, and curiously ignorant. He dined with us one day, and chose, *à p, opos* of nothing, to begin a discussion concerning the evil of the bishops being in the House of Lords, and various other delinquencies and enormities of the Church, including the bigotry of supposing that ordination would make any one a minister unless he was a godly man; that it would be much better to stay and read one's Bible at home, than meet for public worship with an indifferent minister After this, H—— took him to preach at the school, and ordered all the boys to attend. It raised a great disturbance: for, in addition to the preaching, Mr. G——. got hold of a man's lingum, or badge of caste, and took it away; and though he was forced to return it, the whole town has been in a ferment at the insult, and our school is almost broken up in consequence. We have now only twenty boys, instead of forty-five. They are all petitioning to use their own *heathen* books instead of ours, and we have no more requests for admittance."

Without impugning the purity of the motives of the gentleman, this lively lady has given a practical proof of the evil which misdirected efforts, however well intended, are sure to occasion. Dr. Buchanan has remarked the tendency to discontent, which has often manifested itself amongst the British troops in India; and considering that the military body is, in that country, under very peculiar circumstances, that they formerly had few religious advantages, that they were enabled to indulge, moreover, in much sensuality and intemperance, it generated a spirit of independence and indifference to the opinion of the world, greatly at variance with a due regard to military subordination and order. A spark dropped amongst such combustible materials might inadvertently occasion an infinity of mischief.

After the two striking instances we have given of the line taken by very worthy, probably, but certainly very indiscreet men, it is much more gratifying to reverse the picture and give an extract from Pridham's valuable work on Ceylon :—

" Before closing our remarks on the state of Christianity, we cannot refrain from bearing our testimony to the *single-mindedness*, judgment, and truthfulness, which has characterised the missionary body in this colony. They have not, like too many of their contemporaries in the Pacific, the West Indies, and the Cape, added by their own presence a plague to the evils they had come to cure. They have not, like too many of their brethren, deemed a sordid greed, aggression, acquisitiveness, audacious exaggerations, and the vilest hypocrisy, impudent meddling, and vulgar insolence, to be necessary components of the missionary character ! On the contrary, they have practised self-denial in every form and shape, have worked in an exhausting climate with more than superhuman energy, have always under, rather than over, rated their own success ; and have, alas ! in too many instances, left their bones to bleach on the shores of the island they had come to save."

" Prudent and peaceable means of instruction," says Buchanan, " exercised on the multitudes of no religion, or on Christians who scarcely know why they are called

by that name, will not excite to rebellion, but will call
forth, in after years, a general expression of thankfulness
from all parts of India to the British nation."

It would have been fortunate for India had all
the missionaries pursued the same praiseworthy
course mentioned by Pridham. The conduct of
some over-zealous persons amongst them, however,
induced, to a certain extent, a prejudice against the
whole body.   Of this we have a striking proof in an
anecdote related by one who has since been so ho-
nourably distinguished in the Christian annals of the
East, Dr. Carey, soon after his arrival in Calcutta:—

"This morning," he writes, " I went to visit the
Reverend ————, an evangelical preacher of the Church
of England, who received me with cool politeness   I
stayed nearly an hour with him, and found him a very
sensible man.   He carried himself greatly as my superior, and I left him without his having so much as
asked me to take any refreshment, though he knew I
had walked five miles in the heat of the sun."*

In a country where the duties of hospitality are so
universally practised, we can only account for the
very chilling reception Dr. Carey met with from the
good chaplain by the cause we have already stated,
the disinclination that was generally felt towards the
missionaries by the European community of that
day.

* "Memoirs of Dr. Carey," by his Son.

This was precisely the ground taken, in the boisterous debates in the House of Commons, by Mr. Lushington and others, who saw, in the proposed inundation of India by dissenting partisans, a hidden source of danger and disquietude, and possibly the nucleus of some formidable outbreak.

Now we would wish to speak of the missionaries with every respect, particularly those sent out by the Church Missionary Society, to whom Bishop Heber extended his countenance, and whom he describes as " respectable young men, well pleased to find themselves recognised as regular clergymen, and treated accordingly." We know that, as a body, they are highly conscientious men, earnest and sincere, and moreover, generally speaking, that their zeal is tempered by discretion. In the miserably deficient state of the Church Establishment, which prevailed even so late as the prelacy of Bishop Heber, their services could be made, and no doubt occasionally were so, highly useful to the European community, who were destitute of any other minister. But, happily, this deficiency is a matter of " the past," and to be recorded merely as a passing cloud, which cast its sombre shade over " the Church of other days." The chaplain is now to be found almost everywhere, or at least within a convenient distance; and his services have doubtless acquired an additional value, if, in some instances, he has been able by example as well as precept to counteract the misdirected efforts of the irregular auxiliary, overflowing with an exuberant sense of his own importance, and looking with ill-disguised contempt on the more rational and sober-minded practice of our own communion.

" Every inspired cobbler or fanatical tailor," it was observed by Mr. Lushington, in the debate to which we have before referred, "who feels an inward call, imagines he possesses a kind of apostolic right to assist in the spiritual siege which has been already commenced, not merely against the pomps and vanities of the world, but against the more lawful and innocent recreations of life."

The history of modern India bears us out in stating that persons of this description have occasionally worked their way into the barrack-room, and, availing themselves of the flightiness which is to be found in an uncultivated mind when stimulated to religious fervour, have awakened feelings not exactly calculated to uphold authority, by drawing a forcible contrast between their own fanciful standard of ideal excellence and the lives of the officers, and even of the ladies of the regiment. It is here that the chaplain may be most usefully exercised; for here enthusiasm will be more generally found to prevail than in those of the superior classes, and it is accordingly amongst these imperfectly educated but sincere and earnest men that he may be the means of solid good. His superior education, his greater knowledge of the world, his cultivated mind, his polished manners, acquired by mixing in good

society, must always invest him with a certain
degree of authority and weight in checking the
ruder tendencies of the soldier.

A writer in the "United Service Magazine" thus
expresses himself on this subject:—

"I beg also to add, that instead of there being any
prejudice against the parsons, or rather chaplains, of the
army, speaking generally, *they are held in the highest
respect*, more particularly abroad, where their services
are usually most required, there being no other clergyman; and on his being attached to any particular
brigade or station, he is received, both by officers *and
men*, with as much respect as the pastor of any parish
can be. The opinions of an old soldier, ventured in
favour of his class, and speaking according to his conscience, will, it is to be hoped, be favourably considered
by all who value the welfare of the British soldier."

We have a pleasing instance of the correctness of
this statement in the farewell sermon delivered by
the Rev. Mr. Allen, on his quitting the division of
the Bombay army, with which he had served
throughout the campaign in Affghanistan, during
which he appears to have been occasionally exposed
to danger. We learn from his journal that, when-
ever it was practicable, Divine service was regularly
performed; and in this very affecting discourse he
bears ample testimony to the kindly feeling with
which his ministration had been received by both
officers and soldiers. Like his brother chaplain,
Mr. Whiting (whose name has since been so honour-

ably distinguished), he appears to have sedulously availed himself of every opportunity, where the services of a Christian minister could be usefully employed, to advance and uphold his sacred profession.

Previous to 1815, when the late Mr. Thomason, a very exemplary clergyman, accompanied the Marquis of Hastings's camp, there was, so far as we are aware, no instance of a chaplain being employed with troops on service in the field. Indeed the paucity of their numbers, even for garrison duty, precluded it; for we learn that at former periods the services of the chaplains of the Royal Navy were occasionally resorted to, even at Fort St. George, to assist in the performance of the ordinary duties. The East India Company had, it must be remembered, entered into engagements with the Government to provide chaplains for Her Majesty's troops serving in India. Had the screw been put on at the Horse Guards, as it would most probably have been in less exciting times, a neglect of the obligation incurred would not have so long remained, to be ultimately remedied by the force of public opinion, kindled into active exertion by the startling statements of Dr. Buchanan of the total inadequacy of the Ecclesiastical Establishment to supply even the wants of the army.

With the civil and military residents his position is more satisfactory and his duties more easy. He is not condemned to mediæval asceticism; and, eschewing dissipation, his occasional presence at

social meetings will be a security against their
degenerating into debauchery, and will banish
ribaldry and unseemly frivolity. His example will
afford a useful lesson to others, in using and not
abusing the *agrémens* of life; and in proportion to
the respect and esteem in which he is held by the
community will the sphere of his usefulness be
enlarged and extended. We are aware of more than
one instance in which the legitimate exercise of the
influence exercised by his sacred character, and the
result of his friendly remonstrance and advice, have
saved the young officer from a course of early dissipation that would have most certainly terminated
in misery and ruin. And surely here was one step,
and a most important one, gained; for it cannot be
too deeply impressed on the minds of young men
that, setting aside all considerations connected with
a future state, it does not admit of a question, as
regards their prospects of worldly advancement and
temporal welfare, that such portion of happiness as
is attainable here is not, and from the nature of
things cannot be, associated with the indulgence
of unrestrained passions, and with giving the rein
to unlicensed indulgences. Contrast the healthy
frame, the well-braced nerves, the quiet and refresh-
ing sleep of the abstemious, with the feverish and
broken rest, the wild and fanciful dreams, and the
racking headache that, surely as cause and effect,
follow the matin of a debauch ! and the self-control

that has been exercised, when wine and wassail offered strong temptation, will be its own reward.

The Abbé Dubois, than whom none were better acquainted with the tone of feeling and prejudices of the natives, amongst whom he lived for thirty years, says :—

" In what estimation can a Brahman hold men who admit Pariahs into their domestic service, or keep women of that vile tribe as servants, or in a more criminal capacity ? What respect can he have for men who debauch themselves in public, who even appear to consider the detestable act of drunkenness as a gallant feat ? "

We are aware that in attaching so much importance to mere uninspired ethics we shall, by our modern Gnostics, who, hurried away on the fiery wings of a heated enthusiasm, soar into the pure regions of high air, enwrapt in the brilliant coruscations of a mystic and supermundane adoration, be considered as taking very low ground. Be it so. Virtue, as our reason tells us, is distinct from religion ; and the practice of moral self-subjection, however laudable in itself, and however conducive to our temporal happiness, is not all that is required of us. Still we are satisfied that it is a step in the right direction, and that the mind, inured to the rough discipline of self-denial, and accustomed to the healthy restraints of self-control, is prepared, gradually it may be, and by slow degrees, for the

full developement of the intellectual faculties, and
for the consequent acknowledgment of higher and
nobler duties.

> "Let mortals learn this truth,—
> That while they keep to Virtue's narrow path,
> With guards invisible they march surrounded:
> The gods, who surely guide them on their way,
> From this no more than from themselves will stray,
> For Virtue's of Divinity a ray."

We offer no comment on the following extract
from Whitehead's "Sketch of the Established
Church in India," but the respectability of the work
from which it is taken sufficiently attests the convictions of the author:—

"The more worldly politician, conversant only with
second causes, may deem our argument fanaticism, and
pity the superstition which has prompted it; but it is a
notorious fact (and let the infidel or free-thinker account
for it as he may), that neither a ship containing a
missionary has ever been lost between England and
India, nor a station containing a church dedicated to
God's honour and service has ever been in even tem-
porary occupation of the enemies of Britain."

In the former part of this sketch we have traced
from an early period the Church Establishment for
British India, and we now subjoin its present numbers,—

3 Bishops,

3 Archdeacons,

37 Chaplains,

87 Assistant Chaplains; independent of a bishop;

an archdeacon, and several chaplains, stationed on the island of Ceylon, and of a numerous body of missionaries of various denominations.

In conclusion, we feel we cannot do better than subjoin an extract from a charge of Bishop Heber to the clergy of the then Archdeaconry of Madras, on the 10th of March, 1826. It not only most admirably describes the peculiar position and arduous duties of an Indian chaplain, but derives additional solemnity and interest from the melancholy fact that it was delivered but a few weeks before the close of his earthly career :—

" It is, indeed, most true, that those men would be much mistaken who should anticipate in the fortunes of an Indian chaplain a life of indolence, of opulence, of luxury. An Indian chaplain must come prepared for hard labour, in a climate where labour is often death; he must come prepared for rigid self-denial, in situations where all around him invites to sensual indulgence; he must be content with an income, liberal indeed in itself, but very often extremely disproportioned to the charities, the hospitalities, the unavoidable expenses of his situation. He must be content to bear his life in his hand, and to leave very often those dearer than life to His care who feeds the ravens.

" Nor are the qualifications which he will need, nor are the duties which will rest on him, less arduous than the perils of his situation. He must be no uncourtly recluse, or he will lose his influence over the higher ranks of his congregation ; he must be no man of pleasure, or he will endanger their souls and his own. He must be a scholar, and a man of cultivated mind ; for in many of his hearers (wherever he is stationed) he will meet with a degree of knowledge and refinement which a parochial minister in England does not often encounter, and a spirit sometimes of fastidious and even sceptical criticism, which the society, the habits. and, perhaps, the very climate of India, has a natural tendency to endanger. He must condescend to simple men, for here, as elsewhere, the majority of his congregation will, nevertheless, be the ignorant and the poor.

" Nor, in his intercourse with this humble class of his hearers, must he anticipate the same cheering circumstances which make the house of the English parochial minister a school and temple of religion, and his morning and evening walk a source of blessing and blessedness. His servants will be of a different kind from himself, and insensible, in too many instances, to his example, his exhortations, and his prayers. His intercourse will not be with the happy and harmless peasant, but with the dissipated, the diseased, and often the demoralised soldier. His feet will not be found at the wicket-gate of the well-known cottage, beneath the venerable tree, in the grey church porch, or by the side of the hop-ground and the cornfield ; but he must kneel by the bed of infection or despair, in the barrack, the prison, or the hospital.

"But to the well-tempered, the well-educated, the diligent and pious clergyman, who can endear himself to the poor without vulgarity and to the rich without involving himself in their vices, who can reprove sin without harshness and comfort penitence without undue indulgence ; who delights in his Master's work, even when divested of those outward circumstances which in

our own country contribute to render that work picturesque and interesting; who feels a pleasure in bring-
ing men to God, proportioned to the extent of their
previous wanderings; who can endure the coarse (perhaps fanatical) piety of the ignorant and vulgar, and
listen with joy to the homely prayers of men long
strangers to the power of religion; who can do this
without himself giving way to a vain enthusiasm, and
whose good sense, sound knowledge, and practical piety,
can restrain and reclaim the enthusiasm of others to the
due limits of reason and scripture;—to him, above all,
who can give his few leisure hours to fields of usefulness
beyond his immediate duty, and who, without neglecting
the European penitent, can aspire to the further extension of Christ's kingdom among the heathen: to such a
man as Martyn was, and as some still are, I can promise no common usefulness and enjoyment in the situation of an Indian chaplain.

" I can promise him, in any station to which he may
be assigned, an educated society, and an audience peculiarly qualified to exercise and strengthen his powers
of argument and eloquence. I can promise him, generally speaking, the favour of his superiors, the friendship
of his equals, and affection, strong as death, from those
whose wanderings he corrects, whose distresses he con-
soles, and by whose sick and dying bed he stands, as a
ministering angel. Are further inducements needful?
I yet can promise more. I can promise to such a man
the esteem, the regard, the veneration of the surrounding Gentiles; the consolation, at least, of having removed from their minds, by his blameless life and
winning manners, some of the most inveterate and most
injurious prejudices which oppose with them the recep-

tion of the Gospel, and the honour it may be (of which examples are not wanting among you) of planting the Cross of Christ in the wilderness of an heathen heart, and extending the frontiers of the visible Church amid the hills of darkness and the strongholds of error and idolatry. In what I have said, I feel that I have expressed, almost without intending it, my opinion as to what manner of man an Indian chaplain ought to be; and to such of you as fill that honourable rank any further pastoral advice seems scarcely necessary.

" There are two points, however, which I would generally press on the notice of all, because I can hardly conceive a situation in this country where an attention to both will not be most necessary and blessed.

" The first is a continued and earnest furtherance of, and attention to, those powerful aids in your spiritual work, by the bounty of individuals, the parental care of Government, and the pious munificence of the venerable Society for Promoting Christian Knowledge; in regimental or station schools, wherever they exist or can be established; in the dissemination of religious tracts, of our excellent Liturgy, and the Holy Scriptures; and in the arrangement and conduct of those lending libraries, which should more particularly fall under the chaplain's care, and which I hope, by God's blessing, to see established throughout this land, wherever there is a barrack to receive, or a European soldier or invalid to use them."*

We commenced this work with a sentence of the Duke of Wellington's, a name glorious and great;

* *Vide* Note 4.

we trust we could not have concluded it more appropriately than with the rather long quotation we have
given from Bishop Heber, who lived honoured,
loved, and respected, and whose memory will ever
be cherished with tender affection and veneration.
His name, like that of the incomparable Swartz, is
destined to descend to the latest posterity, and to be
chronicled by the future historians of India as one
of those "burning and shining lights," that have at
intervals irradiated that benighted portion of the
globe.   These, which may almost be called his concluding words, charm no less by purity of style
and elegance of language, than as the reflex of a
mind that was never wearied in inculcating "peace
on earth, good-will towards men."   Every sentence
breathes the affectionate interest he felt in the welfare and efficiency of his clergy, and in the moral
and religious improvement of the community at
large.   In short, this Charge may be considered as
a perfect epitome of the peculiar and anomalous
position of an Indian chaplain ; whilst it is beautiful in sentiment, practical in application, and in
spirit, if we may venture to use the expression,
divine.

NOTES.

NOTE 1, p. 11.

THE subjoined extract from a General Order, under date "Ferozepore, December 25th, Christmas-day, 1845," written at the moment of victory after a most decisive and sanguinary combat, is a remarkable proof of the respect paid by Lord Hardinge, under the most exciting circumstances, to the duties of religion:—

"These grateful and heartfelt acknowledgments to the army for its services cannot be closed without humbly remembering that our thanks are due to Him who is the only giver of all victory, and without whose aid 'the battle is not to the strong.'

"The Governor-general therefore invites every British subject at this station to return thanks to Almighty God, this day at eleven o'clock, for the mercies he has so recently vouchsafed us, by assembling at the Governor-general's tent, where prayers and thanksgivings will be read by the Governor-general's chaplain.

"By order,

(Signed) "F. CURRIE."

NOTE 2, p. 27.

It must be admitted, from the many instances recorded by early writers on India, that religion sat but lightly on the European residents in general. It was usual for the higher classes of the society to accept invitations from opulent Hindoos "to festivals *in honour of* the idol"—such being the phraseology on their cards to *nautch* celebrations—which, to the unguarded young and newly-arrived strangers, offered great attractions. It would sometimes happen that these fell on a Sunday evening; and we read, in his "Memorial Sketches,"—"Mr. Brown had too frequently to observe that the congregation of the church was thinned to increase the company attendant on the idol; or that, with still greater inconsistency, some were heedlessly proceeding to these exhibitions from the very doors of the sanctuary, where they had been professing to worship the true God." Some of these visitors, "to gratify their host, were not unfrequently induced to bow the head or bend the knee to the image; pleading, in excuse, that "if they go to the house where the idol is displayed, it is but civil to the person who entertains them to compliment him, in return, with a mock respect for his religion." —*Sketches*, p. 73.

A more recent writer, Lieutenant Bacon, relates a still more curious incident:—"The Begum usually gives a grand *fête*, which lasts three days, during Christmas, and to which nearly all the society of Meerut, Delhi, and the surrounding stations, is invited. I have by me one of her circulars: ' Her highness the Begum Sumroo requests the honour of ———'s company at Sirdhana, on Christmas-eve, at the celebration of high mass, and during the two following days, to a *nautch*, and a display of fireworks.' Here," observes Lieutenant Bacon, " the burden of the exhibition is distributed pretty equally between our good friend the Bishop, the *Nauchsiees*, and the fireworks. Of these spectacles, most who have witnessed them agree that the religious pageantry has the lead in point of display and finery."— *First Impressions in Hindostan*, vol. ii. p. 51.

Those who are familiar with Hindostan will probably not easily forget Julius, bishop of Amatorita, Vicar-Apostolic of Sirdhana, the confessor to the Begum, whom Miss Roberts describes as " realising the most beautiful ideas which could be formed of a Christian minister." Bacon describes the Bishop as " the very essence of a Romish priest;" and Bishop Heber ascribes " his popularity to the smoothness of his manners, and his tact in administering to the self-love of his associates." " The Begum" (we quote from Miss Roberts) " has erected a church after the model of St. Peter's at Rome. Both the design and execution of this cathedral are very beautiful ; the altar of white marble, brought from Sessore, and inlaid with cornelians and agates of various colours, being particularly rich and splendid."—*Scenes of Hindostan*, vol. ii. p. 204.

Bishop Heber, in a letter to Lord Amherst, dated 24th of January, 1825, in speaking of one of these stations, says :—" I was greatly pleased with the church, chaplain, and congregation of Meerut, all of which are more *English* than anything of the kind which I have seen in India."— *Life of Bishop Heber*, vol. ii. p. 281.

Those days are now, as well as most of the actors in them, passed away. But what could have been more painful, to so conscientious a man as the chaplain at Merut, on one of the most solemn festivals of our church, than to observe the seats usually filled, not merely by the gay and thoughtless young officer, or the graver civilian, but even " by the fairest of the fair," unoccupied, and his truant congregation on the wing to assist at the gorgeous and imposing ceremonies of high mass, and at the more questionable entertainments that followed in rapid succession, in this singular combination of Christian and heathen observances ? What construction would be put upon their conduct by the more intelligent of the European soldiers ? and to what purpose would it not be turned amongst the native Roman Catholics, by a man of so much *tact* as the Vicar-Apo- stolic of Sirdhana, who (says Miss Roberts), "from his talents and his amiable character, is a welcome and an honoured guest at the houses of the British residents ? "

We know not whether the Bishop be still alive; but both at Goa and at Pondicherry are to be found ecclesiastics of the Church of Rome, of a superior order, not in rank merely, but in education, in talent, in courtesy of manners, and in *tact*.

Note 3, p. 92.

"A strict attendance on their respective duties must be re- quired of all degrees of officers whatever, not excepting the *chaplain;* which *officer*, well chosen, well directed, and properly employed, might be of notable benefit to an army.

"I would not be misunderstood, or thought so unfashionable as, gravely and dryly, to recommend the service of God to a world so constituted as the present; but the *sneerers* will spare me, when they find that I here advise a constant and regular performance of *divine service* in the field, not purely on a *moral*, but pretty much on a *political account*, and in uniform pursuance of one of my *principal heads*, the good *economy of the army*.

"That *this* is effectually promoted by the means here recom- mended is not, with me, a point of *empty speculation*, but a *fact* confirmed by *experience*. In short, I will venture to affirm (be- cause I have seen it so), that by making your army *better men*, you make them *better soldiers:* and that a *spirit of order* instilled into them in *this* particular point, soon diffuses itself through the whole economy, and will be plainly seen in their persons, their clothes, arms, accoutrements; their conduct, diligence, obedience; and even in their *courage* and resolution against the *enemy;* of which *this* is the firmest and most lasting foundation, let the abandoned, profligate, debauchee think what he pleases. And so come I to a close of this long-winded chapter."—*A short Course of Standing Rules for the Government of an Army.* By a Lieutenant-General of His Majesty's Forces. 1744.

As thought this quaint old writer, so, in more modern times, thought "the illustrious Duke;" and of the justice of their conclusions we will cite only one memorable proof, in the history of the celebrated Swartz, who, we learn from his biographer, Dean Pearson, repeatedly, in the absence of a chaplain, officiated as such to large English garrisons. "It is, indeed, astonishing, if we consider the manners of our troops in India," writes Mr. W. Chambers, one of his most steady friends, "how he has been able to persuade whole garrisons, to whom he sought to be of service, by every means in his power. The kindness of his heart, and the unaffected simplicity of his manners, soon procured him a civil reception among them." "He speaks with much pleasure," says Dean Pearson, "of the soldiers in the garrison of Tanjore (His Majesty's 48th Regiment), who attended divine service both on Sundays and at the weekly evening lectures, which were frequented by great numbers." Connected with this subject, Swartz concludes with a remarkable fact, to which we respectfully invite the attention of those who adhere to the lash as one of the most indispensable auxiliaries in upholding military discipline, although we are not of those who consider that it can be altogether dispensed with:—"To this," attending divine service, "they are encouraged by the officers, *who all confess that corporal punishment had ceased from the time that the regiment began to relish religious instruction.*"

In 1794 we find him, with equal success, officiating as chaplain to His Majesty's 74th Regiment, then stationed at Tanjore, and in the neighbouring cantonment of Vellum. Military readers will recollect the important place occupied by this fine regiment in the annals of Indian warfare, for nearly a quarter of a century; and how gloriously it distinguished itself under the command of the brave Colonels Wallace and Swinton, in the memorable battle of Assaye, on the 23d September, 1803.

Of the characteristic disinterestedness of this very remarkable man, his biographer gives an affecting proof in the following passage:—"While thus adverting to the various charitable labours of this excellent man, it may not be irrelevant to observe, that for a considerable space of time during the late war he forbore, on account of the public distress, to draw the pay which was due to him as chaplain to the garrison. Mr. Hudlestone, in communicating this circumstance to the Government, observes:—'Mr. Swartz makes no other use of money than to appropriate it to the purposes of charity and benevolence.'"—Vol. ii. p. 58.

And yet his means were of the humblest, for Mr. W. Chambers says : — "At Trichinopoly he had much to do, with very narrow means. His whole income *was ten pagodas per month*, or about forty-eight pounds per annum ; and if we estimate it according to the effective value of money in India and in England, it will not be equal to half that sum : I mean, that an European may live much better in England on 24*l.* per annum than he could in India for 120 pagodas."—Vol. i. p. 165.

Can we wonder that the influence of such a character, powerful as it was with the European soldier and with the native convert, by whom he was almost adored, extended yet further, and softened the barbaric heart of one of the most formidable and inveterate foes the British had hitherto encountered ? "The Christian character of Swartz attracted during this perilous crisis universal confidence and esteem : and so powerfully had his conduct impressed Hyder Ali himself in his favour, that, amidst his cruel and desolating career, he gave orders to his officers ' to permit the venerable padre to pass unmolested, and to show him respect and kindness ; for he is a holy man, and means no harm to my government.' "

" He was generally allowed to pass through the midst of the enemy's encampments without the slightest hindrance ; and such was their delicacy of feeling towards him, that when it was thought necessary to detain his palanquin, the sentinel was directed to assign as a reason that he was waiting for orders to let him proceed. Thus, when the whole country was overrun by Hyder's troops, the general reverence for the character of the *good father* (as he was emphatically called), enabled him to pursue his peaceful labours even in the midst of war."—Vol. i. p. 397.

Bishop Heber, in a letter to Wilmot Horton, dated Trichinopoly, 1st April, 1826, thus sums up his character :—

" Swartz was really one of the most active and fearless, as he was one of the most successful missionaries who have appeared since the Apostles. To say that he was disinterested in regard to money is nothing : he was perfectly careless of power, and renown never seemed to affect him, even so far as to induce even an outward show of humility. His temper was perfectly simple, open, and cheerful ; and in his political negotiations (employments which he never sought for, but which fell in his way) he never pretended to impartiality, but acted as the avowed, though certainly the successful and judicious agent of the orphan prince entrusted to his care, and from attempting whose conversion to Christianity he seems to have abstained from a feeling of honour."—*Journey through the Upper Provinces of India*, vol. ii. p. 462.

A marble monument, executed by Bacon, was erected to his

memory by the East India Company, and in the general letter from the Court to the Government of Fort St. George, dated October 29, 1807, we read: — "On no subject has the Court of Directors been more unanimous than in their anxious desire to perpetuate the memory of this eminent person, and to excite in others an emulation of his great example."

It is hoped that this brief notice of the remarkable man, who, during his pious labours, extending over a period of fifty years, so often officiated as a chaplain to the troops, will not be considered out of place in this work.

NOTE 4, p. 113.

There is an anecdote in Wilkinson's " Sketches of Christianity in India," which may be appropriately introduced as a commentary on Bishop Heber's charge :—" What sort of fellows are these," said the late General H., when on a tour of inspection, in reviewing His Majesty's 14th Foot, addressing the officer in command of the regiment, "for whom the chaplain is pleading to build them a private reading-room?—he calls them '*his men.*'" 'The best men,' replied the Major, ' in the whole regiment. I only wish they were all 'his men.' 'Then,' exclaimed the General, 'they shall have their room.' "—P. 264.

London :—Printed by G. BARCLAY, Castle St. Leicester Sq.

www.ingramcontent.com/pod-product-compliance
Lightning Source LLC
Chambersburg PA
CBHW071219050326
40689CB00011B/2374